Intellectual Property on Campus

Intellectual Property on Campus
Students' Rights and Responsibilities

TyAnna K. Herrington

Southern Illinois University Press
Carbondale and Edwardsville

13   12   11   10   4   3   2   1

Library of Congress Cataloging-in-Publication Data
Herrington, TyAnna K., 1955–
Intellectual property on campus : students' rights and
responsibilities / TyAnna K. Herrington.
       p. cm.
Includes bibliographical references and index.
ISBN-13: 978-0-8093-2993-9 (pbk. : alk. paper)
ISBN-10: 0-8093-2993-X (pbk. : alk. paper)
ISBN-13: 978-0-8093-8584-3 (ebook)
ISBN-10: 0-8093-8584-8 (ebook)
1. Intellectual property—United States. 2. College
students—Legal status, laws, etc.—United States.
3. Universities and colleges—Law and legislation—
United States. 4. College teachers—Legal status, laws,
etc.—United States. I. Title.
KF2979.H469 2010
346.7304′8—dc22   2009051728

Printed on recycled paper. ♻
The paper used in this publication meets the minimum requirements of American National Standard
for Information Sciences—Permanence of Paper for
Printed Library Materials, ANSI Z39.48-1992. ∞

For my students

Contents

Preface

It is not the strongest of the species that survives, nor the
most intelligent, but the one most responsive to change.
—Charles Darwin in Richard Florida, *The Flight of the Creative Class*

The quote above is particularly significant for students today, as they face a world demanding fresh approaches to the economy, global environmental stewardship, health care, and the impacts of technologically based communication, among other important areas. They are learning to develop work in a time of great change, and responding to the challenge requires innovation and new directions. It also requires a clear understanding of intellectual property law that affects students' control of their own work, as well as their access to intellectual products that make learning and innovation possible.

When there is demand for new products, innovative creations, and solutions for treating current problems, it is today's students who will be filling that need. And it is of real importance that students realize that the work they create, even while they are students, can form product bases for their careers, as well as intellectual and experiential foundations for social engagement in America's dialogic processes that shape the future. Whereas, in the past, issues in intellectual property law failed to gain the attention of most individuals, new developments in technology that enhance the average creator's ability to publish and use work, among other changes, have brought intellectual property conflicts and consideration of policy to a new level of awareness in many students' minds. And as one author notes, "[u]niversity management of intellectual property has become more aggressive and sophisticated in the last few years, and this has been reflected in an increase in financial returns" (Lee 96). As universities' administrators note the potential value of on-campus development of intellectual products, attentiveness to students' rights in intellectual products becomes more important, both for students and for educators whose responsibilities extend to students' needs. If individual educators became more aware of the impact their own pedagogical decisions can have on students' potential to create useful intellectual products and to benefit from their learning experiences, it would help not only to enhance the educational process but also to eliminate legal missteps when treating students' work; pedagogical choice can carry legal ramifications. I hope this book will help both students and educators understand students' rights and responsibilities while they are in the midst of the academic process. I also hope that students will understand enough of the issues in intellectual property that they are able to use that knowledge long after they've completed their academic endeavors.

This work is not intended to provide legal advice of any kind; in fact, as I underscore throughout the text, legal conflicts develop within singular contexts and must be treated with those specific contexts in mind. Instead, the book provides explanations and illustrations of how the law works and why it is important to creative developers, especially while they are students. It treats issues that I find most important and that my students find most interesting, and it examines those that I believe will best prepare students to deal with intellectual property challenges during their academic careers. The last two chapters in particular discuss the more abstract and complex theoretical issues that drive a unique treatment of student work; I hope they, above all, will help students discover the importance of the work they do while they are in school and help them lay claim not only to the work they create but also to the way it represents them as individuals.

Intellectual Property on Campus: Students' Rights and Responsibilities is useful to students and educators across a broad spectrum of disciplines and interests. Avoiding legal conflicts in university settings, as well as strategizing means to benefit from student-educator-institutional legal relationships, is of common interest to students, instructors, and educational administrators across all academic fields. I focused this work on my own discipline, technical communication, partly because the examples and issues that arise are most familiar to me but also because the work in the field ranges broadly across academic disciplines and can provide examples that will be familiar to those who work outside this particular field. My students work in new media studies, engineering, architecture, computing, business management, and humanities studies, among others, and the material here is directly applicable to their efforts. But, in fact, it is also applicable to the work of students and educators from other fields. And although there is some distinction among secondary education and university settings that vary from small to large state institutions, private academic bodies offering two-year college experience, undergraduate degrees, and graduate and postdoctoral education, administrators will find that the issues noted here apply to anyone working with students.

Moreover, the concerns treated in *Intellectual Property on Campus* are important and applicable even beyond the academic setting. The same issues that I treat in relation to user/creator interplay in educational settings form the base for legal concerns that are applicable to the needs of all creators and users, whether in posteducational experience, in the midst of their educational enterprises, or in the process of considering an educational venture for themselves or for their children. And beyond aspects of the law that may be of interest to each individual personally, the concepts treated here are important in assessing the effects of intellectual property treatment on the state of the nation itself, for all Americans are affected by educational experience; nearly all personally in secondary school, and 45 percent in college-level interactions (Murray). For this reason, the material here provides a base for reflection that should be of importance to a wide range of readers. Beyond this connection, the material in the book can inform all readers, as both users and creators of intellectual products, about the legal issues they may encounter when developing and using innovative work, whatever the venue for that creation or use.

I begin the book with a foundational explanation of the law and how it is treated in my own field of technical communication. The general subject and content of these introductory pages may be familiar to those who have examined issues in intellectual property law before. In this case, I suggest that those readers pass over these pages or read them cursorily. But novice readers or those whose interest is to reacquaint themselves with issues in intellectual property should begin at the beginning.

I encourage readers to maintain equilibrium both in finding means to protect their intellectual products and in tempering their reach in accessing the intellectual products of others. A healthy, robust society requires an educated populace and depends on its citizens to create; these goals call for access to others' works as a base for learning and as a platform from which to build new works. But inventors and creators must find benefit to themselves in the work they create if they are to expend effort, time, and money to develop new intellectual products and to make them available to the rest of society. This book is meant to provide a means for its readers, and students in particular, to explore these issues of balance by examining their potential from perspectives as both creators and users. I hope they gain enough understanding to begin to distinguish between what they may use of others' works to support their own education, critical commentary, or innovation and what use would go too far. And I hope they will begin to understand how they might protect their own works, while still making them accessible enough to accomplish the goals that originated with their initial motivation to create them. In either of these cases, I expect that readers will begin to understand that when using and developing intellectual products, the same laws that may hold them back can also be those that allow them the freedom to learn.

Acknowledgments

Good fortune, friendship, and collegial support have followed me throughout the process of this project, and I am thankful for the support and advice I received during its course toward publication. It has been my good fortune that Karl Kageff at Southern Illinois University Press has managed and guided the project through its multiple stages, and I appreciate his support throughout its development. I am thankful to Wayne Larsen for his careful editing. I am also grateful for Martine Courant Rife's careful and sound review and responses to the manuscript in its early stages. I thank Peter McGuire for suggesting that I pursue this project and for supporting its progress. I also thank Daniel McQuillen for his permission to use his "Icarus guy" image in the book. And I thank my students, whose efforts in creation and use of intellectual products inspired my interest in treating the project's subject matter. Finally, as always, I am especially grateful to Pat and Jack Herrington for their constant encouragement and support of all my endeavors and am ever cognizant of my great luck that they are my parents.

Introduction: Students, Educators, and Intellectual Property

The American Constitution provides an ingenious mechanism for democratizing and optimizing the way that U.S. citizens may control, disseminate, and manipulate intellectual products. When the system maintains balance, it supports a society in which all its citizens can access, respond to, and create political and cultural information, participating broadly in influencing the country's character and future. Within a balanced intellectual property structure, education and new knowledge thrive and new intellectual products proliferate. When the system is balanced, creators of new intellectual products are supported in their efforts; their work benefits both society and themselves. Alternatively, when the structure is imbalanced, either the nation's citizens are prohibited from accessing information for participating in the country's democratic development, or creators retain so little benefit from their work that they forgo efforts to develop new work and society gains little new knowledge.

Balance is also important when considering how to treat students' relationship to intellectual products within academic systems. As a group, students are often characterized infamously in their capacity as users, noted for downloading music from the Internet, copying and uploading video clips to interactive sites such as YouTube, and copying photos, graphic images, and other material from online sites, seemingly without consideration of

1

potential intellectual property law violation. Emphasis on students' assumed illegal use of copyrighted material can make it easy to forget that students maintain rights of access to information under the same laws that allow access to other U.S. citizens. Fair use, personal use, information access supported by the First Amendment, and other constitutionally sustained uses of intellectual products support rather than inhibit use of otherwise protected materials. Decisions regarding legality of use must be determined within a total context of circumstances in which the use takes place, so wholesale prohibition *or* support of intellectual product uses is untenable and ill-advised.

Students also maintain rights to control the intellectual products they create, even in their capacity as students. They both use and create intellectual products, and as is the case with all other users and creators, neither of these rights of access or control is absolute. Just as the law is applied to other creators and users of intellectual products, it is also applied to student uses and creations. In all cases, the context in which creative action or use occurs determines how intellectual property law is applied. But the distinctive context of the academic setting affects students' work uniquely; they create and use intellectual products most often as a means to become educated. They create intellectual work more often as a byproduct of the educational process rather than with the goal of developing a product for some purpose tied to its inherent worth. What issues arise when students' uses of intellectual materials are legally challenged, and how does the academic context affect those challenges? And what issues arise when users, either within or outside the academic structure, violate students' rights to their intellectual products?

A number of articles concern student intellectual property rights in educational settings and treat student work, although they are not directly focused in this area. The topic has been of interest in my field, technical communication, and its related field of composition. Works in technical communication that treat intellectual property law include but are not limited to those of Gurak, Durack, St. Amant, Diaz, Reyman, and Hawisher and Selfe, and many of these authors research both in technical communication and, in particular, a branch of rhetoric and composition, computers and composition. The computer and composition field's leading journal, aptly titled *Computers and Composition*, has dealt extensively with intellectual property and its relationship to students, whereas other intellectual property articles in technical communication have focused more on workplace, pedagogical, or professors' issues (Gurak, Herrington, Durack, Gattis, Giesler et al.). In 1998 *Computers and Composition* devoted a special issue to intellectual property issues as they relate to the composition field. Its topics included publishing and the Web, collaboration in virtual space, copyright in the classroom, course license ownership, multimedia issues, and fair use in relation to the First Amendment. Other issues of *Computers and Composition* have included articles that deal with intellectual property and students. These involve work that includes references or related commentary on student work: "Why Napster Matters to Writing: Filesharing as a New Ethic of Digital Delivery" (DeVoss and Porter) provides an important view of student file sharing. "Was Foucault a Plagiarist? Hip-hop Sampling and Academic Citation" (Hess) brings out many conceptual points that support student use of creative materials to support learning and is helpful for understanding why student use of copyrighted material supports educational processes. Taking a theoretical tack, "Turnitin.com and the Scriptural Enterprise of Plagiarism Detection" (Marsh) examines plagiarism in light of the abstract implications of Turnitin.com as a control mechanism reflecting paternalistic constraints on teaching, document development, and student critical thinking. Researchers who work primarily with composition have also contributed works that are useful for studies in technical communication (Spigelman, Miles et. al., and Logie). "The Fair Use Doctrine: History, Application, and Implications for (New Media) Writing Teachers" (Rife) does analyze student fair use and provides a good starting point for discussing students' rights and responsibilities in intellectual property; this article forms a basis for broader treatment of student product development and intellectual property. Researchers who work primarily in rhetoric and composition also have contributed work useful to those in technical communication (Spigelman, Miles et. al., and Logie). Articles in other fields treat a general set of issues such as these above, as well, but none focus exclusively on students' rights and responsibilities in intellectual products.

To date, few books treat concerns at the intersection of intellectual property law and student work products in academic settings. *Composition & Copyright: Perspectives on Teaching, Text-Making, and Fair Use* (Westbrook) addresses some issues regarding students' intellectual products but again does not focus directly on students' rights and responsibilities. *Intellectual Property: Copyright Ownership in Higher Education—University, Faculty, and Student Rights* (McMillen) explores students' rights issues, and *Computer and Internet Use on Campus: A Legal Guide to Issues of Intellectual Property, Free Speech, and Privacy* (Hawke) centers on intellectual property concerns on campus, but as is the case with *Who Owns Academic Work? Battling for Control of Intellectual Property* (McSherry), which explores issues of product license ownership in academic settings and does treat student work in some sections, these works do not focus specifically on student issues.

It is more important than ever that students and their professors understand how students' intellectual products may be treated under the law. Today many graduate and even undergraduate and high school students display a level of sophistication with technology that surpasses that of many workers active in the business world. Their facility with technology often leads them to create marketable work products based in new technologies and then to pursue entrepreneurial efforts to promote them. When students' work has the potential to be valuable, representatives of their educational institutions may claim interest in student products created within the educational setting. And today, even young students, such as Ben Casnocha, who founded a software company at the age of fourteen and was named "entrepreneur of the year" at seventeen (Hurt), are creating intellectual products of value to the public. Institutional administrators may declare rights in student work, regardless of whether their claims could be supported under the law. Students, their instructors, and their department and university administrators should understand how intellectual products are treated under the law; students should realize they do have rights to the intellectual products they create, and instructors and administrators should recognize the limitations on the claims that they might wish to make on rights to student work.

This book is an attempt to give educators and their students a basis for understanding legal and ethical issues surrounding student use and creation of intellectual products within the academic setting. The focus is particular to the field of technical communication, but research and teaching in technical communication reach into a vast range of other disciplines and both inform and are informed by them. For example, our research in technical communication examines specifically, among a host of other issues, those in computing, digital media, medical communication, engineering, business management and organizations, science studies, law, graphic design, digital games, architecture, gender issues (within many areas), politics and civic structures, and literature and creative writing. Among others, these fields are situated within humanities and social sciences, visual arts, hard sciences, and technology programs.

Using this connection between technical communication and other areas of work and study provides a means to treat intellectual property issues within a specific frame of understanding that I hope will be helpful to my colleagues; but the material can be applied to other subject areas so that it also could be useful to those outside the technical communication field. I hope readers find the material useful across a range of disciplines and venues.

Regardless of field-specific interest, the academic structure is unique in several ways that affect both students' and educators' actions regarding intellectual products:

- Both students and educators use intellectual work extensively in the learning process. The overriding constitutional goal of knowledge advancement in the intellectual property clause plays out broadly in the educational context, so use of intellectual products by students and educators must be understood in light of the foundation for intellectual property law, in both its support of and its limitations on use.
- Students create intellectual products in the process of learning as participants within educational institutions. As such, their work relationships to and within the university setting can create confusion as to how they may be characterized as creators and the extent to which they retain rights in and control of their work.
- By virtue of the educational setting, instructors and their teaching institutions have an unusual level of power over student work and over students' futures. With this power comes both legal and ethical responsibilities that must be considered when treating student work.
- The educational setting is ripe for plagiarism, as well as copyright violation. Some students and educators may conflate issues in plagiarism and copyright law, which can lead not only to misunderstanding but also to potential legal and ethical violations. It is important to mark the clear distinctions between these two treatments of intellectual products so that both instructors and their students understand the legal and ethical ramifications of both.
- Classroom interactions require pedagogical choices that are legal, ethical, and consistent with the teaching goals of each instructor, and instructors should understand the impact of their assignments that lead to students' creation of intellectual products. Problems may occur when instructors choose assignments that are inconsistent with pedagogy and unwittingly lead students to violate rules of ethics or copyright law. For example, if an instructor intends that students learn rote material and, as separate authors, produce discrete products, but asks students to work collaboratively in preparing them, the instructor may confuse students about how singly-authored work is created and could unwittingly encourage students to claim each others' work as

their own. Alternatively, instructors might also make pedagogical or administrative choices that unwittingly violate students' copyrights in their work. For instance, instructors might ask students to produce work that would be used for out-of-class purposes either within the university or in service learning assignments for local nonprofits or businesses. Instructors who demanded compliance, without ensuring that students control their own copyrights, could easily infringe students' copyrights.

- The educational setting is an extremely favorable venue for learning to interact in a democratic society by appropriately using and creating intellectual work to represent ideas and critical thinking. Students can take advantage of the opportunities that the educational setting provides as long as they and their instructors are aware of the rights and limitations under our accepted systems of law and ethics. Understanding intellectual property law can help both instructors and their students successfully participate in their educational communities and as citizens of the country and the world.

Much of this book concentrates on the rights of students in their work, in part because students' rights have been overlooked in recent discussions of intellectual property issues. As such, I focus at times on an approach to student work that seems to advance a "creators' rights" or protectionist direction to intellectual property law rather than emphasizing rights of users in intellectual products. I want to make clear at the outset, however, that I maintain the position I forwarded in my first book, *Controlling Voices: Intellectual Property, Humanistic Studies, and the Internet*, which argues for activist support of rights of access to intellectual products to encourage egalitarian democratic dialogue in the United States. But much as users can be the weaker parties in arguments over public access versus corporate control of information, students are the weaker parties in intellectual property disputes with their professors, administrators, or educational institutions.

The common bond between my approach to students' work here and the thesis in my first book on intellectual property is an overall concern that weaker members of institutions, universities, public forums, or national structures, whether users *or* creators, should not be coerced, repressed, or oppressed by way of intellectual property law.

Copyright and "Copyleft"

Over the past several years, a number of writers who want to broaden the public domain and support the right to access copyrighted material have begun using the term *copyleft* to encourage a licensing choice that allows users to reproduce, use, redevelop, and distribute the copyleft-licensed work, as long as the new work also carries a copyleft license. Lawrence Lessig, a law professor at Stanford University who has written numerous legal documents and law review articles, and who created a blog in support of an access orientation to copyright, has also developed the Creative Commons license, a mechanism by which creators can choose how to protect their work or make it available to others. In addition, Richard Stallman, a computer programmer, created the GNU license, a tool that allows similar choices for treating intellectual product creations in copyleft and the Creative Commons license. These mechanisms strongly benefit society by balancing increasingly restrictive statutory copyright law with the public's need to access and respond to others' work in order to create new products. In addition, the infrastructure that supports these licenses is often educational in nature and leads creators through a process by which they are able to understand specifically their choices for treating their work. Students who work with creative computing and generate new work in digital media, among other creative fields, are often aware of these established licenses, and many find them attractive in part because their use implies a choice to go beyond the realm of standard legal practice for treating intellectual products. These licensing structures are often viewed as retaining a sense of edginess in going beyond the norm.

While I enthusiastically support these means to provide balance and promote public interest and I support the prospects that characterization of a licensing choice as a "dissident" means of treating the law might attract new creators and educate them about their choices, I want to make clear that there is nothing illegal or unsupportable in creators' choices to license their work as desired. Whereas GNU and Creative Commons licenses are effective for those who make use of them, the term *copyleft* can be misleading to new creators or to those who see the term without understanding what it represents. The presence of *left* in the term implies that creators' choices to license their works with a set of access or restriction rules different from what is provided automatically by the copyright statute is somehow leftist, politically radical, or subversive. On the contrary, creators' choices are granted explicitly in the copyright statute. Making use of these choices can positively affect public rights and individual choice in treating intellectual products and could support a more robust public domain. I hope that students will understand their choices as authors, perhaps by way of this book, and realize that they can influence our national perception of intellectual property law, its value as a means to bolster political and cultural dialogue, and its role as a mechanism to support the creation and distribution of innovative work.

Chapters' Content

This book is intended to provide students and their instructors with a basis for understanding how the law might affect their rights and responsibilities in treating intellectual products; it is not meant to offer legal counsel or specific answers to decisions about how to treat intellectual products developed within the educational setting. Nevertheless, it presents pragmatic discussions for understanding and responding to intellectual property law issues as they relate to students' work in educational institutions. Within this general framework, the material makes clear that every legal conflict arises within its own unique context and that one set of circumstances can lead to legal considerations or decisions vastly different from those of a similar set. To illustrate issues regarding the law in application to student work, the book provides a range of potential choices for treating students' intellectual products and discusses the possible results of those choices. The book examines multiple areas of the law that relate to intellectual property and the issues that affect student choices about developing their intellectual products. These include copyright, fair use, free speech, patent, trade secret, trademark, work for hire, joint work, agency partnership, and contract law. Whereas the book is a starting point to understand potential ramifications of the law for student work, students, professors, or their institutions should retain an attorney for directed legal advice on specific cases arising from within their own unique set of contextual circumstances.

In addition to pragmatic application of the law, this book also treats policy issues in relation to students' intellectual product development. It discusses fair use of copyrighted materials to support free speech and educational pursuits and treats this area of the law both in terms of its relation to student use of copyrighted materials and concerning educators' use of materials to support their students' work. The book also discusses policy issues in relation to educators' and institutions' ethical responsibilities regarding student work, particularly in areas where copyright and plagiarism are conflated. Later chapters also assess and discuss pedagogical policy, suggesting means to motivate teaching in directions that could preclude the need to police plagiarism while avoiding violation of students' copyrights. The book ends with this, as well as discussion of pedagogical directions for incorporating sound intellectual property policies in ways that support constitutional goals for advancing learning, supporting free speech, and promoting democratic dialogue.Chapter 1, "Students'

Rights in Their Intellectual Products," explains the different kinds of legal protections possible for intellectual products and briefly discusses their benefits and limitations. It examines the different kinds of protections of students' work in educational settings but focuses on copyright, since student-authored products are more commonly protected under this provision. Issues of authorship and authority are important in this chapter, and so is its discussion of the 1976 Copyright Act, still controlling law today, which forms the base of the copyright law that determines how students gain authoritative control over their work and delineates their rights in the work they create.

The second chapter examines ways in which student collaborations can affect rights in their creative products. Group projects, so prevalent on campuses, both in and outside classrooms, can create unwitting lifetime legal relationships between or among students who choose to work together and find themselves creating products that could be considered joint works. And students who work with professors could face the same potential for joint work development, or they might encounter claims against their work on the basis of the work-for-hire doctrine. Students may not realize the potential that working within or for a university might have for control of their creative products in copyright. This chapter explores that potential and discusses ways that contracts can affect student work relationships with other collaborators or with their institutions, which in turn can affect the legal characterizations of the creative products they develop. Students may also contribute to work in creative ventures that lead to patents, often involving joint partners within the educational institution in which the student participates. This chapter examines issues in patent that might affect students, so that they and their instructors can become better aware of the relationships in these kinds of intellectual ventures.

The material in this chapter also considers the ways that new technologies might broaden the impact on student work in educational settings. For instance, the developing practice of requiring technical communication students to create blogs as part of their classroom assignments opens the door for claims in joint works, both in and outside the academy, and leaves open more possibilities for copyright violation, both by students and of students' work. Learning about intellectual property law is particularly important in light of technological developments that allow global reach from and to student work.

Where the previous chapters center on students' rights as *creators* of intellectual products, chapter 3, "Intellectual Products within Educational Settings," focuses on the rights, responsibilities, and limitations as *users* of legally protected intellectual products within educational settings. This chapter discusses users' rights and responsibilities as they relate to both student and instructor use of copyrighted and trademarked materials. Beyond core concepts in and application of fair use to student and instructor actions in terms of student downloading and the new context of the Internet for using and working with online material, the chapter examines the Technology, Education, and Copyright Harmonization (TEACH) Act and what it means for using material to further learning in educational settings.

In the fourth chapter, "Authorship, Plagiarism, and Copyright," discussion centers on how authorship is created and the different treatments of creators' work in literary and philosophical understanding of authorship, in contrast to legal treatments. It examines ways in which plagiarism is distinct from but related to concepts in copyright. Students, as well as their instructors, may conflate these two characterizations of unauthorized use of others' materials, since they both arise from concepts of authorship. Being aware of the distinctions is important for understanding the potential impact of misuse. This chapter pointedly asks whether using antiplagiarism databases such as the controversial commercial policing agent Turnitin.com is ethical or legal. It asserts that companies that use plagiarism databases and, without permission, use student work as items of comparison in searches for plagiarism violate student copyrights in the process. Discussion in this chapter centers on the legal and ethical problems in using databases such as this and provides counterarguments to protection services' defenses, such as the claim that fair use provides an excuse for their infringement.

The conclusion, subtitled "Legal, Ethical, and Pedagogical Considerations," examines educators' ethical responsibilities to their students and promotes approaches to treating student work in a way that minimizes educators' influence and control over student products. It also addresses students' ethical responsibilities to their peers, instructors, and institutions. Finally, it completes the book by discussing new cultural developments in the ways that students and their instructors treat intellectual products, both as users and as creators. Cultural changes in how we understand authorship and authority affect the ways we assess the value and control of information, and the conclusion discusses means by which these changes can impact students' and educators' choices and change the educational system as a whole. More to the point, it argues for pedagogical choices that coincide with how we value information early in the twenty-first century. Today, education should not be grounded in routine acts of information memorization, which, by nature focuses on noncontextual material that can be copied—or plagiarized—but should offer means for contextualized learning, developed in stages with incremental advances in understanding and critical thinking so that students assimilate understanding of their subjects rather than reproduce rote information.

I want this book to provide a basis for students, professors, administrators, and the nonacademic public to understand how intellectual property law can impact students' intellectual product use and development in academic settings. I hope that after reading this book readers will consider their roles as actors in treating and creating intellectual products as means to enable their activities as participants in dialogic practice, whether in academia or in democratic systems.

1

Students' Rights in Their Intellectual Products

The ideals that the Framers embodied in the constitutional provision treating intellectual property are particularly important to academic practice. The primary goal of the provision is to support learning and to advance knowledge creation, and the academic enterprise epitomizes these goals. Explication of the intellectual property provision, sometimes called the "copyright clause," demonstrates that the Framers chose to illustrate their intention to support learning as a primary goal by employing a rhetorical structure that makes the benefit to the author secondary and merely supportive of the primary goal. This was a significant choice at the time of constitutional development because it distinguishes U.S. law from European law. Where European law, then and today, supports the "moral rights" of authors, making authors' protection of their work primary, American law contrasts by instead making primary society's goals of educational advancement and the related democratic access to information.

Moral rights are those connected directly to authors and their reputations, in that their work is representative in nature. Because these rights are personal, they cannot be transferred, bought, sold, or modified but are attached to the author. Among these are the right to claim authorship of a work, to prohibit another from claiming authorship, and to prevent the work from being modified so as to protect the actual author's reputation. In contrast, American law provides authors with rights in their work as a means to support a greater policy goal of advancing learning and supporting a democratic society.

The Constitution's intellectual property provision states, "The Congress shall have the power . . . to Promote the Progress of Science and the useful Arts, by securing for limited Times to Authors and Inventors the exclusive Right to their respective Writings and Discoveries" (U.S. Const., art. 1, § 8, cl. 8). To help ensure that the goal is met, the Framers fashioned a means to motivate authors by providing an incentive of benefit from the work they create. This incentive, different from a physical property right in a tangible object like a cow or cottage, comes with limitations that ensure a focus on knowledge development as a primary goal. Authors are limited both by the duration that they are allowed to retain rights in their work and in the power that this right is given—the benefit exists only because it supports the overriding goal of extending knowledge development. This second limitation takes many forms, which are discussed later in this chapter and later in the book, but is most visible in treatment of First Amendment rights and both personal and fair use, which provide intellectual product users with access to work otherwise protected by copyright. The limitations ensure that a public domain of information exists as a foundation for making new knowledge to strengthen the country. The Supreme Court stated this explicitly in *Williams & Wilkins v. U.S.*:

> Copyright is not primarily for the benefit of the author, but is primarily for the benefit of the public. The copyright law makes reward to the copyright owner a secondary consideration, and the courts in passing upon particular claims of infringement must occasionally subordinate the copyright holder's interest in a maximum financial return to the greater public interest in the development of art, science and industry. (1345)

The Framers were ingenious in developing a mechanism that would guarantee expansion of the country's knowledge foundation based on the input and interaction of new ideas that grow from existing ideas, while simultaneously supporting democratic dialogue necessary to forward egalitarian access to information to allow national participation in molding the country. For the intellectual property provision to work well, a constant balance between users' and authors' interests must be maintained. The general U.S. citizenry, with its interest in participating in democracy by accessing information as a basis for free speech, among other supporting features of self-actualization, is characterized as users, and the overall policy behind the Constitution furthers their interests. Authors' and creators' benefits are supported by law rather than policy. The graphic shown here visually represents the balance between users' and creators' interests.

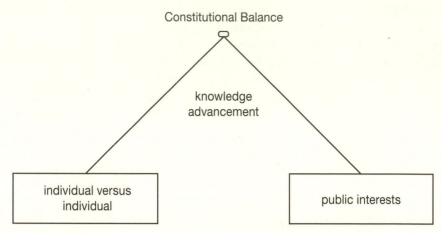

Balance of public access and creator's benefit to support constitutional policy

The Constitution's policy to support knowledge development provides the fulcrum on which the public's and creators' rights are balanced. The overall structure of this balance, the policy behind it, is treated through legislative action, and our representatives are charged with ensuring that constitutional intent is reflected in the statutory laws they pass. In intellectual property law, questions regarding policy, which are tied directly to interpretation of intent in the Constitution, are always focused on the balance of users' and creators' interests. But in most circumstances, conflicts in intellectual property occur at the legal level, when interests of one creator are pitted against those of another and legal questions are answered by assessing facts and applying legal statutes.

Simply put, *policy* is interpreted by creating law that should be consistent with the Constitution; *legal conflicts* are resolved in the courts by assessing facts and applying the law through the process of trying cases. The overall emphasis on law means that the Constitution's policy and its need for support are often ignored.

Students find themselves in activities that place them simultaneously on both sides of the policy fulcrum. They are not unique in their characterization as both users and creators of intellectual products, but the extent to which they act in both capacities is broader than for most of the general public because they are required to use and produce intellectual products as everyday activities in educational settings. As users, students face the same limitations that affect the rest of the public as intellectual property law becomes more restrictive. For instance, when the 1998 Sonny Bono Copyright Term Extension Act was passed, it changed the term of creators' copyright control from life of the author plus fifty years to life of the author plus seventy, and for corporate authorship, from seventy-five to ninety-five years from the date of publication. The extension has caused the public domain, and therefore access to information and to materials from which to build new knowledge, to shrink. Works that would have become a part of the public domain—and could have been used as a basis for building new knowledge—are now kept from public access. The extension act was passed immediately before Disney's Steamboat Willie character, along with thousands of other works, would have entered the public domain. In addition to extending protection for new works by twenty years, the act allowed a twenty-year extension of renewal terms for works published before January 1, 1978, thereby making unreachable until 2019 intellectual products that previously would have been earlier available to the public.

The current term of copyright is so lengthy that new works will not enter the public domain within the lifetimes of most of the people who live during the lifetimes of those who create them. In addition, other new laws such as the Digital Millennium Copyright Act and the TEACH Act, examined later in this book, support protectionist interests in intellectual products, limit access to intellectual products, and forward a protectionist approach to information.

That corporate lobbyists were powerful in generating these changes is significant. Large corporate holders such as Disney and the Gershwin Foundation, and powerful multimillionaire individuals such as Bill Gates and the late Michael Jackson acquired vast numbers of copyrights in works that would have become part of the public domain if the extension act, titled the "Mickey Mouse Copyright Extension Act" by dark humorists (West), had not passed. These copyright holders control information that forms the base of who and what we are as a society. They can choose who is allowed to use these materials and who is not, effectively controlling speech and inhibiting public dialogue. On the scale of balance between users' and creators' rights, when corporations control large amounts of information, hampering the benefits of access to society, the scale tips far out of reach of a balance that would further the Framers' intent to advance knowledge and support a democratic society.

To provide a modicum of balance, rights in free speech and fair use (examined later in this book) do provide some basis for supporting the public's interest in intellectual products despite the new limitations in intellectual property law. And "two centuries of judicial interpretation of the Intellectual Property Clause and the First Amendment have established the public's interest in 'fair use' of copyrighted material" (Sharp 6). But access to intellectual material has become difficult, in part because the reach of intellectual property protections is broad, and in part because facing corporate entities' legal teams to pursue rights to use their intellectual products is daunting. These limitations, coupled with the emphasis on court cases that, by necessity, usually treat issues of law rather than policy, inhibit legal public access at the turn of the new century.

The significance for students is that developing their work within the academy is, for most, one of the rare instances where gathering intellectual material for critical comment and examination to support learning is the focus of their daily efforts. Without access to a full public domain their educations are limited. In addition, learning within a system in which limitation to educational material is accepted and considered acceptable can imprint students with a frame of mind that can lead them to acquiesce to limitations on access as a normal part of their concept of learning within our society. It is not only possible that they would carry this concept with them and limit their potential to create new knowledge once they leave their academic settings, but they might leave the academy accepting intellectual limitations that hamper their access to a democratic process of interaction. Educational institutions should be optimal places for learning and practicing the art of democratic interaction.

The Supreme Court has not directly contended with questions about how fair use plays out in academic settings, but *Williams & Wilkins v. United States* treated the issue peripherally. In this case the Wilkins Company, in conjunction with the National Institutes of Health and the National Library of Medicine, provided complete copies of medical journals to staff members to help them develop research projects and gather general information. The amount of copying was substantial, beyond two hundred thousand pages. The publisher claimed that fair use would not allow the extent of copying and that it was commercially harmed by it. But the Court stated, "There is no inflexible rule excluding an entire copyrighted work from the area of 'fair use.' The extent of the copying is one important factor, but only one, to be taken into account, along with several others" (1345). And it noted, "It is wrong to measure the detriment to plaintiff by loss of presumed royalty income—a standard which necessarily assumes that plaintiff had a right to issue licenses. Such a conclusion results only if it is first determined that the photocopying is 'unfair'" (1347). The significance of the Court's assertions is not only that it highlighted the importance of educational settings for allowing broader use of copyrighted material but also that it underscored that fair use must always be decided in context and that there are potential contexts when even large-scale use of copyrighted work could be legally supportable.

Balance is necessary to reach the goals of the intellectual property provision. As noted above, when powerful entities maintain control over information, limiting access by those who might be inhibited to speak to and participate in society's dialogue, an unhealthy imbalance is created. And just as users can be in a relatively weak position against corporate holders of information, students, *as creators*, can hold a weak position against instructors or institutions who might use their work without permission or make claims against the work they create within their educational institutions. Regardless, under U.S. law, authorship gives students rights to control their work, notwithstanding that it is created within an educational context. But determining student rights to creative products can be complex and cannot be decided without an understanding of the context in which they create work. Students interact within their academic settings in varying roles: sometimes while producing assignments for or within classes, at other times as partners with other students on campus in non-education-related projects, as joint project developers in campus-based collaborative teams, or as student assistants to instructors researchers, or even corporate entities as part of a work-study program. And they may work individually or jointly to produce any number of different kinds of intellectual products. Both the roles they play and the kinds of products they create affect their potential for authorship and thus their control of the work they create. So understanding the bases of their legal relationships to information, either as creators or as users, can help students make solid choices about how they want to treat their work.

Intellectual property law provides a number of different types of protections for varying kinds of intellectual products. These protections include trademark, trade secret, patent, and copyright. Within their educational institutions, students can create or contribute to the development of products that will be protected under these legal categories. For instance, when students work within a campus institute that develops products under secured circumstances, such as they do at the Georgia Tech Research Institute on my own campus, they may be privy to developing concepts that the institute protects with trade secret. Engineering, computing, business and management, architecture, and biomedical departments, among scores of others, also develop projects that can be protected by patent. Students who work with these patentable products could contribute to the extent that they retain or should retain an interest in the patented product that they help develop. Students may also contribute to development of trademarks for special projects on campus, in interactions with other students in common entrepreneurial efforts, or in their capacity as work-study students, among other possibilities. Where students might participate in creating products that can be protected by the modes listed above, it is guaranteed that they develop copyrighted work in the process of attending academic institutions. Copyright is by far the area of intellectual property law that affects them most directly and most broadly. The material in this chapter explains the different kinds of protections available in intellectual property law, treating trade secret, trademark, and patent briefly, and examines copyright in more detail. (See Herrington, *Controlling Voices*, chapters 1 and 2, for more detailed explanation of all areas.)

Trade Secret

Trade secret protects intellectual products exactly as its name indicates. Under the Uniform Trade Secrets Act,

> (4) *"Trade secret"* means information, including a formula, pattern, compilation, program device, method, technique, or process, that: (i) derives independent economic value, actual or potential, from not being generally known to, and not being readily ascertainable by proper means by, other persons who can obtain economic value from its disclosure or use, and (ii) is the subject of efforts that are reasonable under the circumstances to maintain its secrecy. (§ 1, cl. 4)

A uniform act, such as that noted above, is a law adopted by states but created by an external body, usually of governor-appointed private lawyers, area-specific practitioners, judges, and law professors. The uniform law has legal effect only when it is adopted by the state, so students should note whether their states have adopted the act. To date, only the District of Columbia, the U.S. Virgin Islands, Massachusetts, New Jersey, New York, and Texas have not adopted the act but instead use common-law bases for treating trade secrets.

Under the Uniform Trade Secrets Act, individuals who disclose trade secrets can be liable for the damages that result from revealing them. Students should be aware that they may be in precarious positions as participants in projects in which trade secrets exist, particularly as current developments in trade secret law have focused on student manipulation. The most obvious way to recognize a trade secret is when it is the subject of a nondisclosure agreement, making it mandatory that the student agree not to divulge it. But students might not sign nondisclosure agreements and yet may have access to trade secrets. If they see in-house documents that are labeled "confidential," "classified," "private," or some other clear notation of secrecy, students will still have a duty not to divulge the information, even without a nondisclosure contract. Notations of "draft" or "work in progress" may also signal that the materials should remain secret. In addition, if a student knows that the information is the basis for potential profit for his or her employer, he or she should be prepared to treat it as a trade secret. And if the student happens to come across otherwise secured material by accident, the likelihood that its content is a trade secret is high. Because supervisors and coworkers usually treat those who work with them with a higher level of trust, coworkers, even in unpaid internship positions, have a duty not to misuse that trust by disclosing secrets. As such, students should err on the side of caution when presented with the occasion to disclose employment-related information.

Clearly, students who might be given special insights into company processes to aid their educations should not misuse the benefits of their status as novices to violate a company's trade secrets. But students whose learning processes in independent research allow them to uncover negative characteristics about a company or its business should not be punished in the process of learning. Cited as "the darkest secret of corporate India" is a situation in which "several Indian companies are stalking B-school campuses and hiring students with the sole aim of gaining trade secrets of their rivals" (moneycontrol.com). In an interesting case, two computer science students had planned to present research regarding flaws in Blackboard Transaction System's software at the second annual InterzOne Conference to demonstrate that software such as Blackboard's can contain inherent security flaws. Blackboard filed a restraining order against the students and, in an attempt to intimidate them, threatened criminal prosecution under the Digital Millennium Copyright Act (DMCA), even though it was clear there was no basis for the claim. (See also Cohn re: *Felten v. RIAA* and *EFF Felton v. RIAA Audio Files*.) In addition, among numerous other claims, Blackboard maintained that if the students were allowed to present its software flaws at the conference, they would also violate the company's rights in trade secret. For Blackboard to have a preliminary basis for the claim in trade secret, the company must have maintained a secret, and there was clear evidence that it did not. Blackboard's claim was baseless, but the company was still allowed to intimidate students through its legal attacks. The conflict was settled under circumstances in which there was "no indication that the students had the necessary resources to negotiate a fair settlement, any more than they did to defend the original lawsuit"

(Jenkins). This case illustrates that even when students work through research and presentation to support educational progress, their efforts could be subject to serious legal consequences. Students should be aware but not afraid of the consequences for divulging a trade secret.

Trademark

Students also have potential to create or use trademarked products as they move through their academic careers. Trademark provides protection for words, symbols, or sounds that represent a person, company, or institution. The value in trademark is tied to the reputation and goodwill of what or whom it represents, and for the trademark to characterize its subject, it must be a unique and distinctive identifier. A symbol can be used as a trademark only if it does not describe an attribute of more than one company. For instance, the word *hybrid* could not be used as a trademark for a car company that builds hybrid electric-gasoline engines because several car companies make hybrids and the term would not distinguish one from the other. Trademarks must be registered to provide legal protection, and registration creates advantages for registrants, both in procedure and in that earlier registration contributes to an assumption of right to use the trademark.

Students have rights to use trademarks under constitutional free speech and fair use, discussed in the second chapter of this book. But they also retain rights in the trademarks that they produce, even as students in educational institutions. At their best, educational settings motivate students to create and to become excited about developing and using ideas that they encounter in classes or in interactions with other students and professors outside the classroom setting. When students are sufficiently stimulated, they often generate entrepreneurial concepts that lead to product development. Like any other creative products, these benefit from trademark representation.

Students who wish to trademark their creative products must choose unique symbols, words, or sounds that represent them clearly. To ensure that the mark has not been registered by another creator, they must undergo a search process to examine existing trademarks through the U.S. Patent and Trademark Office's Web site at http://www.uspto.gov/. Once students find that the trademark they would like to use to represent their products is available , they must register it with the trademark office. Conflicts would arise if a university claimed that its reputation and goodwill, more than the student's, are attached to a trademark. Once again, the determination would have to be based on the total context of the situation;

it is all the more beneficial, then, that students understand the bases for trademark before creating one. Some examples of university complaints against students include *New York University [NYU] v. Barry Edwards* and a case pursued by Full Sail Inc., a technical college, against Ryan Spevak. The 1996 dispute between NYU and Edwards involved Edwards's use of "nyu" as a domain name in his Web site "www.nyu-law.com." Edwards, then a first-year law student, was able to learn experientially from his interactions with the university, when he received a cease-and-desist letter demanding that he take down the site on the basis of trademark infringement. In part, the university concern surfaced because Edward's site included links to "cybererotica" that was accessible in three to four clicks from the NYU-inspired domain name ("NYU Student Pulls Website").

The conflict between Edwards and NYU was settled without going to court, but other universities took note. Many universities include language within their policies that clarify a stance on use of university names and symbols. Monmouth College's policy is illustrative:

Use of Monmouth College Name or Logos—2008–2009

Reproduction of College Name or Logos—Monmouth College owns exclusive trademark rights to the Monmouth College name, corporate logo, athletic logo and college seal. Vendors wishing to reproduce the College name or logos on commercial products must first obtain a license through the College's licensing agent, the Licensing Resource Group, Inc.

Use by Students or Student Organizations—Any use by students or student organizations of the Monmouth College name or logos on printed or promotional material without advance approval by the College administration constitutes trademark infringement and is subject to legal and/or disciplinary action. Students or student organizations wishing to use the Monmouth College name or logos on printed merchandise are also required to use a licensed vendor. A list of licensed vendors is available from the Office of College Com-munications, ext. 2314.

Implied Use of Name—Trademark infringement applies not only to the unauthorized use of the college name, but also to the unauthor-ized implied use of the college name. For example, a T-shirt produced in conjunction with any Monmouth College–sponsored event or ac-tivity (e.g., Scots Day) must receive advance institutional approval, even if the Monmouth College name or logo does not appear on the shirt [and even if extant law may not support this inhibition; see the third chapter treating First Amendment issues, for example]. (http://www.monm.edu/life/residence-life/scots-guide/use-of-monmouth-college-name-or-logos.aspx)

Technical communication students, as well as those in graphic design, computing, journalism, and as illustrated above, law, among others, work closely with electronic communication, have ample opportunity to implicate their universities through use of their names, and sometimes affect university reputations in their expressive works. Where dilution, the use of the mark in such a way that inhibits others from associating the mark with the trademark owner, is less a problem in student cases, in contrast, student use of university trademarks has the potential to taint the reputation of the school itself, as was the base for complaint in the NYU case. But universities and other learning institutions do not carry an absolute right to inhibit use of the university name to avoid the potential for taint.

In the case of *Full Sail, Inc. v. Spevak*, Ryan Spevak, a former student of Full Sail, a technical college, criticized the college in his Web site with the domain name "fullsailsucks.com." After Full Sail sued to stop Spevak's use of the name and his criticism, both a federal court and the World Intellectual Property Organization, which acted as mediator in dispute treatment in its next stage, found that Spevak was within his rights to criticize the college. The suit was ultimately settled, but Spevak's attorney noted "that similar cases often end in settlements in which 'the little guy has the right to free speech'" ("LA College Files Defamation Lawsuit").

Patent

More frequently than ever before, students are developing highly marketable and sometimes patentable entities during their educational careers. Larry Page and Sergey Brin's Google, developed as a research project while they were students at Stanford University; Shawn Fanning's Napster, notorious but successful, developed while he was a student at Northeastern University; and Mark Zuckerberg's Facebook, created while he was a student at Harvard, are all examples of the kinds of highly popular and marketable student products that have had a positive impact on the Wall Street economy in recent years. When those products are patentable, universities' and students' contributions often become mixed, which leads to legal consequences for both students and their universities. Not only students but also the professors and administrators who work with them would benefit from clear assessments of their legal relationships before entering into them. This section on patent provides a base of information from which to begin.

Katherine Durack has explored patent in technical communication, noting the relationships between the patent and scientific publishing processes. She points to the differences between authority in the ability to disseminate new knowledge through scientific publication and the processes in which patent allows authors to acquire legal ownership of produced innovations. Despite the recursive relationship between scientific publication and processing patent development, the subject of patents is significantly focused in functional product creation rather than idea dissemination.

Patents are used for new processes, machines, mechanisms, or objects, or for improvement of those that were previously developed. To obtain a patent, the registrant must prove that the item or improvement is novel, nonobvious, and useful. When creators determine that these requirements are met, they can enter the process of registering patents in their intellectual products. It would be the rare student who is able to patent an intellectual product without a partnership with a wealthy entity or individual. The patent process is extremely complex and extensive and usually requires a patent attorney's help. As a result, the process is also expensive. An Institute of Electrical and Electronic Engineers (IEEE) publication, for example, notes that "[f]rom start to finish, the average price of a U.S. patent ranges from US $5,000 to $25,000, depending on the complexity of the invention. A reexamination proceeding can cost each side $10,000 to $100,000, and oppositions will almost certainly cost more, since a much wider range of evidence will be considered" (Frank).

For good reason, this potential for expense may lead students to choose university partners in cooperative relationships. When students and faculty enter relationships aware of their choices, the patent development process can be beneficial not only for institutions but for all participants involved.

Many universities create guidelines for distributing patent rights in products that students, professors, and institutions create jointly, and in this case, all inventors must apply for patents jointly. Different universities apply differing guidelines for distribution of income from patented items that they support. The Georgia Tech Office of Technology Licensing within the Georgia Tech Research Corporation (GTRC) provides the following:

> The current distribution of net income is approximately one-third to the inventor(s), 17% to 33% to the inventor(s) "unit," e.g. college, GTRI [Georgia Tech Research Institute], etc., and the balance to GTRC. The share of the income retained by GTRC is firstly used to meet the costs of OTL's [Office of Technology Licensing's] operations, including patent costs on those inventions which are not successfully

commercialized, and any balance is used to further the Institute's research activities. ("Policies")

The University of Minnesota's intellectual property policy provides no specific guidelines for distributing rights in patents obtained jointly by faculty, students, and the university (University of Minnesota, "Intellectual Property"). The Virginia Commonwealth University uses a complicated structure for determining how patent benefits are distributed. Where there are two or more creators, they share equally in royalties unless they have contracted otherwise—and unless the university manages the development cost and protection of the intellectual property. In this case, the university retains 67 percent of royalties in overhead. The remaining net royalties, after costs, then would be distributed in equal shares to the university and the creators. Stanford University's policy includes a 15 percent deduction of patent royalties to be provided to the university to cover overhead costs, then allows that royalty income be divided one-third to the inventor, one-third to the inventor's department (as designated by the inventor), and one-third to the inventor's school (Stanford, "Policies"). In all cases, universities provide for differing structures where independent researchers, labs, or funding sources of any kind participate in patent development. Percentages of royalties provided to independent participants vary, depending on the breadth of their contributions.

Clearly, universities create differing guidelines for how they treat patent benefit distributions, but most make direct statements indicating that their policies apply to students. And in most cases universities retain most of the royalties that result from joint products' patents. Therefore, students should be aware of their universities' policies before entering into creative relationships with them, and they should consider the potential benefit of the work they provide in university settings. Nevertheless, they should also realize that there are advantages to developing patented products with university participants. Beyond the benefit that universities can offer in bearing the expense of patent processing and protection, educational institutions also provide expensive equipment and personnel to support the product development process. They can also be a means to connect with external research partners for funding and information sharing. Partners can include corporate, governmental, or private sources.

By far the greatest difficulties that arise in patent situations are in attributing rights to students and their professors when they develop patent work together. The common structure within universities is one in which graduate, postdoctoral, and sometimes undergraduate students work with professors in research groups. Professors guide teams by providing a direction for the research, in part because they have broad educational background and experience in the research area but also because they have experience with the patent process, as well as connections with funding agencies who support the work. Professors normally write grant proposals with other professors to secure funding, but they sometimes involve students in the grant-writing process. In most situations, the professors have responsibility for including names of participants on the research report and eventually the patent, representing contributions (Seymore 139).

The arrangement is helpful for all the parties involved, and when it is balanced and reflects the efforts of all parties of the group, all benefit:

> Everyone involved in academic research has something to gain. The graduate student receives research training, the all-important letter of recommendation, an academic pedigree, and an elevated status in the scientific community. The professor publishes the fruits of the research, which forms the basis for tenure, promotion, increased funding, the recruitment of additional group members, and prestige in the academic community. The academic department bolsters its reputation and ranking by having a research-active faculty. The university receives valuable overhead from the funded research projects as well as the prestige and ancillary financial benefits that accrue from having academic departments populated with research-active faculty. (Seymore 131–32)

When parties to research groups find that their contributions are not recognized or that they are precluded from receiving benefits from the work they contributed, the structure of mutual benefit fails and conflict arises. Patent law in 35 USC 102(f) makes clear that all inventors must be properly named on a patent for it to be valid. And when a court finds that one or more of the contributors to a patent was not listed, it will invalidate the patent, making it unenforceable. Despite an early tendency for courts to favor university claims against students, *Chou v. University of Chicago* has changed legal thinking and direction. In this case Joany Chou was a graduate student working with her professor, Bernard Roizman, at the University of Chicago. In 1991 Chou and Roizman successfully developed a vaccine against herpes simplex, and Chou asked Roizman how to proceed in applying for a patent for their work. Roizman told Chou that the vaccine was not patentable, and they continued working together amicably for five years. Their relationship changed in 1996 when Roizman approached Chou and told her that if she did not resign he would fire her. Chou continued to work for Roizman, not taking him seriously because they had maintained a close and amiable working relationship for an extended time, but later Roizman barred her from the research lab and told her never to come into the lab again. Confused by the situation, Chou investigated and learned that Roizman had filed a patent on their vaccine in his name alone in 1991 at the time that she had asked him about the patent potential. Initially, the district court found that Chou had no rights in the patent, since she had assigned her rights to the university through a written agreement and that Roizman owed her no duty to support her rights as his student. But the federal circuit court reversed the holding when it found that Chou did have a rightful claim in the patent and held in her favor. The court noted that as her mentor, guide, and friend, Roizman had the highest duty to his student, which required him to treat her with loyalty. This case makes clear that despite signing agreements to forgo their rights to benefit from research contributions, students can still prevail on claims to those rights.

In a narrowing ruling after the Chou case was treated, the University of West Virginia prevailed against its student, Kurt VanVoorhies, when the district court found that VanVoorhies had taken advantage of his expertise and training in patent law to attempt to gain rights in patents to which the university had claims (*University of Virginia v. VanVoorhies*). This case is distinguished from Chou's, since VanVoorhies was the more powerful party and had misused his power to gain unwarranted benefits.

Corynne McSherry points out that patent law's requirement that all inventors be listed on valid patents provides an equalizing structure in regard to students that copyright does not (McSherry 182). But she indicates that it may be the rare student who has the power to pursue this requirement. She notes,

> More often, inventorship, like authorship, is closely allied to academic hierarchy. Because the inventive act is parsed into two components—conception and reduction to practice—and only the former marks one as an originator, the legal discourse of invention maps easily onto the relatively common sense that students and technicians follow the direction of a principle investigator.

So the principle investigator, almost always the professor, has the true power to make decisions about and claims in the intellectual product. And, implied in McSherry's discussion, professors are most often inventors because they usually come up with the original idea and students usually operate in roles as technicians rather than true coinventors (183). Students and professors both should consider their roles carefully and note their inventorship or authorship expectations before they begin work together.

Author or Inventor

Another issue that must be treated before considering patent claims is whether a student has an interest in a patentable idea as an author to a paper about it or as an inventor of the mechanism or discovery itself. The distinction is important because students' intellectual products in these two cases are attributed with differing legal status and are provided with different kinds of legal protections. Students who take part in conceiving the patentable object can be included as inventors, and an invention can be a joint collaboration. Coinventors are not required to work together physically or at the same time, to provide the same type or amount of contribution, or to contribute to every aspect of the patentable object to support a claim as coinventor (Seymore 136). But they must have clearly conceived the idea, the process that reflects the idea, and the end product before pursuing work that supports it. If a professor, rather than a student, envisions the idea and processes, then asks a student to work on it, the student would have no claim to coinventorship. And courts have noted that authorship does not create a presumption that the author of an article contributed to a patent (*In re Katz*; but note that the court did hold that Professor Katz's students did have a valid claim to patent benefits on other grounds).

Students who are not coinventors on projects may nevertheless participate in writing articles about the concepts that support them and even about aspects of the processes themselves. In these cases, students would have claims in copyright to their contributions to publications, separate from any claim in the patent. Lacking a valid claim to coinventorship does not preclude a claim to copyright.

Power and Fiduciary Duty

Technical communication researchers have long worked with analyses of power constructs, in relation both to communication issues and to pedagogical choices within learning venues (i.e., Baker and David, Bushnell, Ding, Kienzler, Kinsella, Richardson and Ligget, and Tillery). And in varying ways, authors in technical communication support learning and development that allow students greater power to make choices in educational settings while learning to gain power through critical ability in preparation to enter workplace settings.

While the works above examine the role that critical thinking and pedagogical support plays in bolstering students' efforts at empowerment within classrooms and in the workplace, in contrast, in educational settings where students participate in patent development, the locus of power is most often in the professor, and students' critical abilities or attempts to gain power are not likely to inhibit their professors' overarching control. Professors have greater power than students to pursue patent work, since their jobs are often tied directly to patent development. In contrast, students' responsibilities are primarily to take classes and participate in research as a part of their education. Nevertheless, students can contribute both patent work and ideas, and when it happens that students do these things truly in conjunction with patent development, they have a legal right to make a claim to their contributions, despite assignment of rights in work to the university.

The validity of student contributions was acknowledged in *PerSeptive Biosystems, Inc. v. Pharmacia Biotech, Inc.* After finding that a student's inventorship was left out of a patent application, the court stated that "[b]ecause the district court correctly found that the named inventors of the patents made material misrepresentations regarding inventorship with intent to deceive the PTO during the prosecution of the patents, we affirm the holding of inequitable conduct" (1317). It is in the best interests of a university, its professors, and its students to make sure that their patent applications correctly identify all inventors, students included, to avoid patent invalidation.

Patent development on campuses usually is based in social structures where teams or pairs of students and professors rely on each other to invent new products and support their successful interactions within common disciplines. Professors maintain valuable connections with funding sources, granting agencies, and business entities that can both support the patent and development process and provide employment for successful students once their academic careers are complete. And they provide students with advice and aid in learning to pursue research activities. Students, in turn, provide inexpensive work support for research and project development and sometimes supply valuable ideas and consideration of project problems. These settings often involve long hours of work between and among students and professors and lead them to rely on each other for support in their joint efforts. Technical communication pedagogy, for instance, can involve service learning in areas where patentable project development has potential. In these instances, students, their professors, and their business associates for which they work in service may all have an interest in product development, and students' interests may be considered less supportable by those who do not see them as full actors in product creation because of their service roles, even though close interaction could lead to equal partnering for product development. More particularly, students may look to their professors for advice and help in the process of professionalizing before they enter the workplace. As noted in the Chou case, the professor may have a fiduciary relationship to the student, requiring a special duty of care in treating student work. So when students have grievances regarding their mentors' behaviors, they may find it difficult to pursue recourse.

Students can use the court system to support their claims to patent contributions, but such action is rare because courts "respect" the inner workings of university research group systems and because graduate students are usually required to assign their interests (Seymore 127). But also students rely on their professors and universities to support their job applications and to provide connections to granting agencies and other funding sources that would support their future work. The inequality in students' and professors' power can be problematic when contributions to valuable patentable objects are being assessed. The different outcomes of the Chou and VanVoorhies cases illustrate that a student's knowledge and power in relation to the patent process can be determinative in considering whether a students' claims are valid. Chou was dependent on her professor and relied on him as a mentor; he took advantage of her reliance to benefit from her work in her stead. VanVoorhies, because he wielded special knowledge of the system, did just the opposite and misused his university's patent structure to benefit in ways that were not supportable.

Some suggest that universities should explain to students how they may pursue patenting processes within academia, and some universities do provide such training. In the right environment, training sessions can be helpful, since students can be creative in response to their course materials. For instance, my own students have shown direct interest in generating ways to provide wireless power to drive electronic devices, thus developing digital toys, game interfaces, and educational software, and they could benefit from broader understanding of patent law and the process of working within the university to develop their work. But the practice can be problematic when university representatives, often trained by their departments and influenced by campus legal offices, provide sessions that focus on meeting the institution's own goals of retaining patents to all products created on campus. Students' interests in retaining rights to their work and benefiting monetarily from their contributions can be underrepresented or even subverted.

Students who consider partnering with institutions in the development of patentable products should note all the considerations above and weigh the relative benefits and detriments in working with their institutions. Regardless of choices that students make, it is important that they understand that they do have options in how to treat the products of their labor, including the option to wait until after they graduate to develop potentially profitable products.

Copyright

By far, more than any other kind of legal protection, students will encounter circumstances in which their intellectual products and the products they use are affected by copyright. The 1976 Copyright Act, still controlling law today, provides instruction to determine what categories of intellectual products can be protected. Procedures, processes, systems, methods of operation, concepts, principles, or discoveries are not covered by copyright protection (in part, because they are treated in patent law). And particularly important in educational settings, copyright protects expression of ideas but not the ideas themselves. In addition, the protected product must be fixed in "a tangible means of expression" (§102[a]). This means that the object of copyright must be perceivable, reproducible, or communicable. Included in the categories of products that can be copyrighted are musical works, literature, dramas, pantomimes, choreographies, films, photos, graphics, sculpture and other artwork; audiovisual work, digital or otherwise; sound recordings; and architectural works.

In class work, homework, special projects, and collaborative development, students create many different kinds of copyrighted work. Most common are the papers they write for classes, but technical communication students also develop class assignments in the forms of Web sites, films, photographs, artwork, digital games, and Weblogs. Students in other fields often create poetry, multimedia art, architectural plans, music, and theater or film scripts, among many other kinds of copyrighted expressions. All of these are protected by copyright. In addition, students may create protected derivative works. Derivative works are intellectual products that are based on an already existing work (but are not considered transformative). For example, a book may be an original work on which a movie is based, and thus the film is a derivative work of the book. The book's copyright holder has the right to create the derivative work or to license another to create it, so a derivative work created independently from the copyright holder's permission would infringe (violate) copyright and would not be legally permissible. The statute of limitation for copyright, the maximal period of time in which to bring suit against an infringer, is three years from the date of the last infringing act.

The 1976 Copyright Act significantly changed the law that existed in its predecessor, the 1909 Copyright Act. The 1976 act makes explicitly clear that copyright protection does not extend to ideas. This limitation is important because it reflects the constitutional goal to support knowledge development; the structure of this limitation on information control ensures that knowledge can flow freely in society so that others can both use it and build on it. The free flow of ideas is particularly valuable in academic settings where students, as well as their professors, are directly engaged in multiple enterprises that further knowledge making. Of course, plagiarism restrictions regulate the ways that and extent to which academic participants can use others' ideas in developing their own. These issues are treated in the fourth chapter of this book. Nevertheless, that ideas are not copyrightable is significant. Students who understand an idea can build from that idea to create new thought, new expressions (that are copyrightable), and new inventions (that are patentable).

Students respond to the needs of society often while they become excited about their work during processes of learning. Being able to use ideas provides students with a base for dialogue, not only limited to the educational setting but within communities, states, and the nation. Ideas embody cultural content, and exposure to varying concepts about life, law, religion, politics, art, science, and other areas of cultural construct opens students to a variety of intellectually stimulating and broadening learning opportunities.

Another significant aspect of the 1976 act, especially for students, is that copyright registration is no longer required for creators to gain protection for their copyrighted work. Under the previous 1909 law, authors were able to claim copyrights only after making valid registrations with the U.S. Copyright Office. Since the 1976 act was enacted in 1978, authors gain copyrights immediately, as long as their products are "fixed in a tangible means of expression" [explained above], even if the work is poor quality. Nevertheless, copyright holders gain advantages when they register their copyrights. Among these are the provision of legal notice and the ability to recover attorneys' fees if they win legal conflicts in which their copyrights are challenged.

Many students, educators, and administrators are unaware that creators gain an "automatic" grant of copyright in their work. Because they misunderstand the law, some assume that students' work is controlled by the institutions in which they produce. But students do retain copyrights, and thus the control that goes with them, when they author works, even within academic settings. The copyright act delineates rights to creators, even in their capacity as students, owing to their characterization as authors or copyright holders. Students, like other authors, have the rights

(1) to reproduce the copyrighted work in copies or phonorecords;

(2) to prepare derivative works based upon the copyrighted work;

(3) to distribute copies or phonorecords of the copyrighted work to the public by sale or other transfer of ownership, or by rental, lease, or lending;

(4) in the case of literary, musical, dramatic, and choreographic works, pantomimes, and motion pictures and other audiovisual works, to perform the copyrighted work publicly;

(5) in the case of literary, musical, dramatic, and choreographic works, pantomimes, and pictorial, graphic, or sculptural works, including the individual images of a motion picture or other audiovisual work, to display the copyrighted work publicly; and

(6) in the case of sound recordings, to perform the copyrighted work publicly by means of a digital audio transmission. (17 U.S.C. § 106)

Although subject to constitutional and fair use limitations, discussed in the fourth chapter, these rights are exclusive to copyright holders, which means that students can prevent educators or their universities from using, distributing, performing, displaying, transmitting, or creating derivative works from their copyrighted work without permission. Universities maintain varying sets of guidelines and policies on student work, and many of these claim rights to the work that students create. But none of these policies or guidelines carry the force of law, and they cannot, in themselves, be used as valid legal claims on students' intellectual products.

In addition, the copyright act makes clear that facts cannot be copyrighted, but a specially created database that contains facts can be protected by copyright (*Feist Publications, Inc. v. Rural Telephone Service Co.*). So even if a student project is merely a compilation of facts but one that is presented in a unique, particularly interesting way, the work can be protected.

The legal validity of students' rights in their intellectual products can change when students develop joint works or become employed within their educational institutions, and their relationships in these capacities can change the ways in which their work is characterized. Whereas this chapter noted problems that arise when students work with professors in patent processes, the following chapter presents a distinctive set of difficulties that arise in copyright when students work collaboratively, either in the classroom with other students and their professors or outside the classroom with other students, with their professors, or for their institutions. Aspects of the law that treat these issues—joint works, work for hire, and the effects of contracts—are discussed, and students' collaborative efforts are examined as they relate to copyright law.

2

Legal Effects of Student Collaborative Efforts

Beyond their individual efforts on projects within academic settings, students also work collaboratively with other students; their professors; corporate, government, or private-project contributors from outside the academy; and, at times, administrators. Their potential to control the intellectual products they develop is dependent on the context of the way in which their contributions are created. Technical communication pedagogy has long supported collaboration among students in the classroom. Early research in teaching through collaboration made use of Mary Lay and William Karis's now classic *Collaborative Writing in Industry* as a basis from which to build. And currently, extensive sources treat collaboration among students, including James Dubinsky's *Teaching Technical Communication*, Stuart Selber's *Computers and Technical Communication: Pedagogical and Programmatic Perspectives*, Cynthia Selfe's *Resources in Technical Communication: Outcomes and Approaches*, and Kelli Cargile Cook and Keith Grant-Davie's *Online Education: Global Questions, Local Answers*, among a host of other books and articles. Because collaborative work is central to student activities in technical communication, as it is in student work in other fields, it is important to note the potential for legal questions as they relate to collaboration.

Areas of law that apply in cases of collaborative development are joint work, work for hire, and contracts. But numerous extralegal factors also affect the ways in which student work is treated in educational settings and can ultimately have a more powerful effect than the law does. This chapter considers how student contributions are treated within the academy and examines conceptual understanding that grounds actions regarding student work. It also explains the legal effects of joint work, work for hire, and contracts on student work projects.

Students often work closely with faculty members, with each other, and sometimes with their institutions in the capacity of employees. When more than one author creates a work, as would be the case in these collaborative situations, participants will develop a "joint work." The joint work issue can create particular difficulty in academic settings, where students work closely with professors to create projects that range from those in which students develop a substantial amount of work and provide important substantive ideas, to those in which students provide rote materials and have no creative input in determining the content or outcome of the final product. And in cases where students receive such benefits as work-study funding or tuition waivers, the authorship, and thus copyright ownership, of a work can be difficult to determine. Students may look to university policies to help determine a basis for how their work may be treated, and they may refer to contracts that they create within the organizational units within their universities. Students' contracts should be available on file within their departments, schools, colleges, or university offices, and guidelines are usually posted in university handbooks, available online within university Web sites.

The complexity of the situation in which students operate as workers, as well as students, is compounded by unequal power relationships between students and professors. As noted earlier, in the description of student-professor relationships in patent product development, professors often provide access to potential employers through long-developed connections and are sources for recommendation letters and evaluation of students' work that can affect their lives both during and after their educational careers. The differing roles of students in collaborative activities can affect legal characterization of the work that they produce, so it is important that both students and professors understand the potential impact of the work practices they undertake.

Joint Works

Students who work with other students, professors, teams, organizations, administrators, or individuals outside the academy and combine their contributions into single intellectual products create joint works. The base concept behind joint work is that multiple parties create an intellectual product with parts that are sufficiently merged so that the product as a whole cannot be represented without all its parts. For instance, the film *Finding Nemo* is copyrighted as a whole even though it contains multiple different elements produced by hundreds of authors. The film includes the graphics that represent the characters, the actors' voice work, the musical score, and the computerized movements that support the graphics, among many other contributions to the whole. When two or more authors develop a joint work in a multimedia project such as this, which combines music, graphics, photography, and coded design elements to create the totality of the final product, both or all retain the copyright in their work and all parties to the joint work must agree to its legal treatment. The copyright in a joint work belongs to all its authors. But each author may agree to contract for a benefit in lieu of copyright retention. Or, under circumstances where a contributor is working as an employee within the scope of his or her duties, the contribution may be a work for hire (explained below), so the individual who contributes it may not have a right in the copyright. In the case that the work is joint and its authors do not dispense with their copyright otherwise, all parties to the joint work must agree if they decide to license it, display or perform it, or treat it in any number of the categories of copyright treatments noted in the first chapter.

In cases where the separate contributions of joint authors can stand alone as individual works, the authors retain copyrights in their individual contributions. So, for instance, unless otherwise contracted, Thomas Newman, the composer who provided the musical score for *Finding Nemo*, would also have retained his copyright in the music, separate from the work as a whole.

Joint work authors have to provide an independent, original contribution to a work to acquire joint author status. Relatively minor contributions such as proofreading or repairing the technology that enables work production are not enough to qualify a participant as a joint work author. So students who do not provide substantive portions of work would not be likely to obtain status as authors. But to gain rights in a joint work, authors are not required to make equal contributions. A student who contributes a substantive portion of work, even when it is of unequal weight relative to other portions of the work, would still be likely to retain joint work status. Without a clear agreement otherwise, each author would retain an equal share in the benefits from joint work.

Joint work authors remain accountable to each other in light of their jointly held copyright for their lifetimes, and if any author has a spouse in a community property state, the spouse could also retain a right in half of the benefits from the work, so other authors might also be legally bound to the spouse as well.

Students who contribute substantially to jointly developed products should be aware that they have potential interests in the benefits of copyright provided in the work. They can have significant interests in a joint work if they provide text, sound, graphics, or even substantial computer coding to allow meaningful substantive connections among elements of a digital product such as those provided by companies like Industrial Light and Magic, which was responsible for visual effects in films such as *Star Wars* and *Pirates of the Caribbean*. Students can also contribute to joint works in engineering or medical research in the forms of reports or academic papers. They may also contribute to joint works in administrative Web sites or departmental publications. In fact, in any jointly developed project in which any other members of the university community would have potential copyrights, students would as well.

Limitations on this potential, beyond the possibility for contracting to provide the work without benefit of copyright, come in work-for-hire application, where students are working as employees for their academic institutions and producing work that is within the scope of their duties. Meeting these two requirements qualifies the university employer to claim a corporate authorship and supersedes the potential for a student to retain copyright in the work. In fact, in the relationship between an employee and employer under work for hire, there would be no joint work.

Work for Hire

Under the legal fiction of *work for hire*, delineated in the 1976 Copyright Act, a corporation or other business entity can be characterized as the "author" of a work for purposes of copyright, even when the work may be created by an individual. Thus, under work for hire, a corporation can gain the same legal status as an actual author for purposes of controlling copyrights. But, for "corporate authorship" to occur, a creator must be legally determined an employee of the corporation, business, or institution and he or she must have created the work for hire within the regular scope of his or her duties. To satisfy these two seemingly simple elements for work for hire requires complex analysis of the contextual situations surrounding creators' relationships with their companies and the products they create. In a conflict over copyright control, a court would first determine whether the creator was an employee by applying agency-partnership common law definitions. These require that a conglomeration of thirteen elements be adequately satisfied, and they include the following, provided by Supreme Court reasoning in *C.C.N.V. v. Reid*:

- The hiring party has a right to control the manner and means for creating the product.
- A certain level of skill is required to produce the work.
- Where a hiring party provides instruments and tools to create the intellectual product, the court will find support for determination of a work for hire.
- If the hired party worked at the hiring party's place of business rather than his or her own, this element will lead to a more likely finding of work for hire.
- The longer the duration of the relationship between the two parties, the greater the possibility of a work for hire.
- When the hiring party assigns additional projects to the hired party, he or she displays more control and is more likely working in the status of employer for purposes of work for hire.
- The more discretion the hired party has over when and how long to work, the more likely he or she is an independent contractor and can maintain control over the work.
- Hired parties who are paid by the hour, week, or month rather than by the job are more likely to be employees.
- When a hired party has a role in hiring and paying assistants, he or she may be legally determined to be an independent contractor.
- If the work created was something usually within the realm of the hiring party's business, this element could help make a showing that the work was not a work for hire.
- When a hiring party is not in business at all, it is harder for him or her to claim to be an employer.
- Hiring parties who pay benefits to hired parties are more likely than not to be employers.
- Hired parties who are taxed through the hiring party's business are more likely to be employees. (*C.C.N.V. v. Reid*)

Students, in their capacity as students, could never be categorized as employees. As students, they are not paid *by* the university but instead *pay* the university to be guided in developing their intellectual products. Other than assigning tasks for classes with guidelines for how their work will be graded, students' professors do not oversee when and where students work. Moreover, students are not assigned class projects as a part of a business endeavor where the students create products from which the university can profit; rather, the goal of their work production for classes is to help them learn. And even though students may use university equipment to create their class projects, unless they are hired specifically in the capacity of employees, their copyrights remain their own. The overall mission of education is not to hire students to produce profit-making products for educational institutions, and it would be absurd to consider that student product development for this purpose could be the regular course of business of a university. But at times students do create intellectual products from which an educational institution could profit, and at these times some representatives of some institutions become interested in how they might benefit from the work that students create on campus, even in their roles as students.

Technical communication students, as well as an increasing number of students from other fields, work to develop creative products by way of their educational endeavor. They may even surprise themselves as they hone their abilities to develop useful, high-quality works. For example, students may develop software for task automation of rote activities; they may create digital films, graphics, or Web designs; or they may write marketable music, dramas, or literature. Some institutions make claims on all intellectual products that students develop during their academic careers. But these claims on student work do not operate as law, and if students can show that their copyrighted work was created outside the realm of a work-for-hire relationship with the university and that they did not willingly contract to provide a license to their work to the university, then obliging students to sign agreements that provide their institutions with rights to their work would most likely render them invalid.

Students' status as authors of copyrighted material also becomes complicated when their roles as students are ill-defined. When they participate in work-study programs to learn from the work they undertake, they may actually be working as employees rather than students. Some students may work for professors whose own work has been funded by a private agency. In this situation, the funding agency might claim a student's product as work for hire. In most cases, the educational institution would have developed a clearly drawn agreement with the funding agency for how the work should be treated and students who participate in work of this kind should understand the arrangement before agreeing to participate. Every student's status, whether as employee or as student, must be determined within the unique context of his or her given situation. There is no single absolute answer that applies to all students' work arrangements.

Even when it has been determined that a student is working as an employee for his or her educational institution, someone who claims that a work was done for hire must still show that the intellectual product was created within the scope of the student employee's work duties. To be within the scope of duties, employees' work must fit the descriptions provided when they were hired, or they must be working within the capacity of growth descriptions provided as they progress through developmental ranks within their job histories. Students may be hired to do very simple, tedious tasks such as answering phones and distributing mail as student assistants, or they may be hired to participate in complex research studies in which their expertise is valuable to the institution. The more rote or mindless the work, the less likely it would be that students could support a claim in their work. But if students provide well-considered products that require special skills or attributes for development, such as those of well-educated technical communication students, they are more likely to be able to pursue arguments in conflicts over whether they could be categorized as employees for purposes of work for hire. In either case, students not only must be employees but also must be creating work that is within the scope of their duties for their intellectual products to be works for hire.

When students create work that they are specifically hired to complete or perform, there is usually no conflict in copyright claims. But at times, students who are hired to provide work to which the educational institution has valid copyright claims instead or in addition create intellectual products outside the scope of their duties. In this case, the work would not fall within the category of work for hire; thus universities could not claim corporate authorship. For instance, a student employee who is hired to create a Web site for an academic department and produces the expected Web site would create a copyrighted work for hire, and the university would be the copyright holder. But if the student also created a digital film about the department, particularly if he or she did so using personal equipment and worked away from campus, the university would have difficulty making a valid copyright claim. Creating the film would not have been within the scope of the duties for which the student was hired, so a university claim most likely would fail. The additional facts indicating the student's independent use of equipment in his or her own work locale could also provide evidence that for purposes of creating the film, the student is not an employee. When conflicts arise and are treated in legal settings, courts must examine the total context of student work development to make decisions regarding employee and work-for-hire status.

Difficulty arises with student employment because the lines between students' roles as students, employees, and individual workers become blurred in academic settings, where students are sometimes "customers" who pay universities for learning opportunities and sometimes employees who provide services. And when learning and working processes conflate, it can be difficult to determine which aspect of the students' work was created as part of the learning process and which was created to fulfill job requirements. To clarify work arrangements between and among students, their professors, and institutions, it is wise for all parties to create and agree to their roles through contracting, so that all participants in endeavors to develop intellectual products clearly understand who controls the rights to intellectual products and to whom product development will be attributed.

Collaboration on Special Projects

There are times when students collaborate on special projects either in classes or in extracurricular activities with campus organizations or with faculty or administrators within their departments. When projects are part of planned organizational activities, students may have a better sense of the role their contributions will play in the special projects, but even then, knowing exactly how their work will be treated, legally and ethically, will help them decide on the extent to which they would like to participate. So when students provide graphic images, video material, text materials, or other kinds of intellectual products to support organizations' activities in the form of brochures, for example, if they intend to retain copyrights in their materials, they will be best served by creating clear agreements to that effect before proceeding. Students may consider the potential value in their work not while they are in school but only after graduation, when they may find that their educational institutions prohibit its use. For instance, a student might create an image to represent an organization's special event or a special project in his or her department. Without a clear agreement indicating who retains control of the image, the organization or department might claim that it is representative of its program and might want to prohibit the student creator from using it in his or her work after leaving the educational institution.Rights to a single contribution to a work can be separated from rights to the work as a whole. So where the totality of a collaborative project might leave a copyright in the hands of the organization that sponsored the work, as explained above, a student might choose to retain the rights to his or her contribution to use in another way or in another project at some other

41

time. But without an agreement to this effect, although not impossible for a student to retain rights in his or her work, it could be unclear as to who would retain control. Clarity regarding these matters is nearly always easier to achieve before a project begins than after it concludes.

Collaborative projects often involve complex legal relationships among the multiple contributors to collaborations. One such complex collaboration illustrates the different legal treatments of work within one project. The image of "the Icarus guy," was used to represent the Icarus Project developed at the Georgia Institute of Technology in 1997–98.

The project was created as a locally based, online technical communication course to teach classes of two hundred or more students about the concepts and principles of technical communication. The course specifi-

Icarus Project illustration. Created by
Daniel McQuillen; used with permission.

cally focused on the contextual nature of communication, especially as it is treated in the discipline. Since the students' instruction was provided only through the online interface, the challenge was to create a structure that would emphasize the nonstatic, contextual nature of technical communication principles within a necessarily static, unidirectional delivery system. Two professors and one graduate student, funded as a graduate research assistant, collaborated to create the resulting online course. One professor, whose field is technical communication, acted as the project director and provided the idea and direction for Icarus, as well as most of the content material for the site. The other professor was the liaison to the university department chairs whose students would take the course in this static fashion. This professor, whose background involves a long history with the institution and respect of his colleagues, not only provided feedback regarding needs and expectations from affected departments but also contributed some content material.

The graduate student provided knowledge and skills to make the technology operate, and created the visual interface for the project, including the "Icarus guy" illustration. The project included three major sections, the first a fairly standard information section and the second a more creative examples section in which students could mouse over hot buttons in a pdf example document and view textual commentary regarding the effectiveness of the document. The third section was the most challenging to create and the most unusual. It provided pdf files of example documents with a description of a contextual situation describing the users of the document and its purpose. Students could then "redesign" the document to fit the context by clicking on radio-button choices to make immediately visible changes in the document. So for example, if a student chose to change cartoon-style images to charcoal-drawing-style images, he or she could click on the choice and immediately see the change. Then after all the choices in a document were made, the student could submit the document as a whole and receive an automated textual response indicating how well or poorly the choices fit the users' needs within the described contextual situation. All three of the Icarus Project's collaborative participants drew on different kinds of unique skills, knowledge sets, backgrounds, and creative thinking to make the project possible, and it would not have come about without any one of the three participants' contributions. None of the participants made an agreement for how to treat their contributions, so in a case where questions arose regarding copyright control, there would be no definitive answer to rely on. Discussion follows regarding issues that would have to be considered in this situation.

The collaboration among the three participants led to one copyrightable product in the online course. But the content provided by the two professors and the illustrations, such as the Icarus guy, provided by the graduate student could all be copyrighted separately. Questions, then, would have to be answered regarding the potential claims of copyright control in the Icarus product as a whole and in each severable portion of the work. The university might claim supportable rights to the project as a whole on the basis that the professors contributed to its creation as part of their regular duties as employees for the university and because it provided the graduate student with monetary benefit specifically to do the work on the Icarus Project, making his contribution a work for hire. But the law is not clear regarding professors' work for hire (see Herrington "Who Owns My Work?"), so there is some possibility that the work as a whole might not be a work for hire in terms of the professors' contributions.

The professors' severable, individual contributions in course content would be even less likely to be considered works for hire, based on treatment of academic work regarding "professor exceptions." (This issue, a topic for another lengthy discussion, is not within the scope of consideration focused on student issues but has been treated in other work. See, again, Herrington, "Who Owns My Work," and extensive treatment in Sandler; Laughlin; McSherry; and Packard.)

In addition to considering copyright control in the work in its entirety, it would be necessary to determine who controls the copyright in each separate part of the project, because each individual's separate contribution could be severed and stand alone from the whole. As noted above, most likely, the professors would be able to retain their copyrights in the course content they provided (see Sandler; Packard; and Laughlin). But it is more difficult to assign copyright control to the student's contributions. The student created the mechanisms that make the Icarus Project site operate, and because this portion of the project is mechanical and developed from software code that already existed in open source in combination with other formats, it would most likely not be considered copyrightable subject matter. But he developed the code in unique combinations to allow him to create programmable pdf's in a way that had not been done before. And he created the illustrations for the project, in particular, the Icarus guy. The university might claim that it holds the copyright to the code and image because the student was working as an employee for the department and created them within the scope of his duties. And if the image represents a university project in a way that is associated directly with the university to the extent that it affects its reputation, it could have an even stronger claim.

The university might potentially trademark the image, and rights in trademark, discussed in chapter 1, would follow. But the form and style of the Icarus guy was based on the student's previous work as a graphic designer, both created before he entered the university's graduate program and used while he worked on his degree at the university. His creative efforts display a unique style that is his own and represent him as the author of works in this style. In addition, the Icarus guy was never an essential aspect of the design but provided a decorative marker. The university never filed a trademark in the image, and its representative quality in the university is doubtful, so the likelihood that the university could make a claim in the image is low. As should be clear, the complexity in deciding authorship and control in collaborative products makes it difficult to understand easily how to apply legal treatment. Contracting could help to avoid the potential for conflicts in the future.

To allow students to be more certain about how contributions to collaborative projects will be treated, they and other participants in product development could create an agreement providing clear intentions for dealing with the work to prepare for potential conflicts. Because each situation in which people collaborate to create intellectual products occurs within its own specific context, the circumstances could be different from those above and would lead to different analysis and legal results, so it is helpful to create specific agreements that fit the unique circumstances of each collaborative endeavor.

As the example above illustrates, collaborative enterprises can be complex and understanding how to apply the law can be difficult, even when each individual goes into the arrangement expecting to provide material for the educational institution. But there are many instances when students find themselves creating work for their departments or academic organizations without a plan to do so. Sometimes sheer enthusiasm for a project or ideal is enough to motivate a group to create intellectual products such as Web sites, departmental project reports, brochures, blogs, management plans, and sometimes even special studies within a program. Technical communication students, as well as others with communication interests and skills, may be intrigued by opportunities to contribute those skills and feel good about their potential to provide work that is seen as valuable. When students contribute to these kinds of projects, ideally, they will understand how their contributions will be treated and they will ultimately benefit from the work they provide. But there are times when students' work is taken for granted.

One former PhD student at a large state university (not my own), now an activist, described her experience in brainstorming with her professor about how they and their department could build a training model for graduate students who were unsure about how to research their projects. She became excited about the idea of a training model and created a framework, a pedagogical plan, and a brochure, illustrated with graphics, to explain the process, then left it in the department's main office for the professor's review over a semester break. When she returned, she found that the professor had used her plan, printed it professionally, and distributed it in his name without her acquiescence and without crediting her with her contribution. When she learned about this and complained that the work was hers, she described the response from the professor as "You're not getting it. You don't exist" (Anonymous interview, May 27, 2007). (See the conclusion for discussion of ethical issues regarding students' work.) Thankfully, this is an extreme example of how students' work can be treated with a documented arrangement, but even minor offenses or misunderstandings regarding collaborative arrangements about product development can lead to negative outcomes. So again, avoiding conflicts over document contributions by coming to clear agreements before creating the work can alleviate problems in the long run.

Contracts

When students do retain copyrights or have potential interests in patented or trademarked products, they can contract with educators, administrators, or their educational institutions to decide how their intellectual products should be treated. To make a valid contract, the parties must all be adults and must have mental capacity to enter into an agreement. In addition, all parties to a contract must enter into it freely. If a court finds that any party agreed to act, not to act, or to provide rights or economic benefit to another under duress, the contract would be considered invalid. In fact, to make a valid contract, parties to a contract have to know what they are agreeing to do, not to do, or to provide. They have to freely make the agreement, and there has to be some kind of benefit to both (or all) parties to the contract. Each party must have the means to bargain for terms of the contract. In cases where a party to a potential agreement has no means to negotiate terms or has such a weak position against other parties that he or she must agree against better judgment or desires, courts can invalidate the contract on the basis of "adhesion clause." Adhesion contracts are often invalidated when courts find that to support them would be unconscionable. The classic example of an adhesion contract is the statement on a ticket for a roller coaster ride noting that purchase of the ticket is tantamount to holding the provider free from liability for injury. Courts will refuse to uphold contracts where they decide that parties did not really intend to agree to all the terms but had so little bargaining power that they agreed nonetheless.

Upon entrance to universities, many students are forced to sign agreements that indicate that the university retains all rights to students' work. These "agreements," which are created in situations where student have no real bargaining power, could be determined unenforceable on the basis that they include adhesion clauses (*Carr v. Signa Securities, Inc.*; *Kugler v. Romain*; and Kessler; also see Herrington *A Legal Primer*, for more extensive explanation regarding contracts).

Teaching Assistantships

Some graduate students in technical communication work collaboratively with their professors as research or teaching assistants. When research assistants contribute more than just monotonous support such as source gathering or calculating numbers to report statistical data in studies, they may have rights in their contributions, as discussed in the first chapter. Graduate students in technical communication, as well as other fields, also take on responsibilities as teaching assistants for undergraduate students in their disciplines. In some cases, graduate students oversee student work in labs, while their professors teach lecture classes, and some provide support for lecture classes by helping with grading and organizational duties; but in some disciplines, graduate students teach their classes independently. There are also instances when students provide teaching materials for the professors they assist; these can come in the forms of notes, Web pages, PowerPoint support materials, and even digital video presentations. When students use professors' notes as content and create frameworks of delivery for them, the likelihood that students would have any copyright claim in the work is low unless the framework itself is a unique original expression. But where students independently develop pedagogical support materials that professors use for their own teaching, particularly in creative formats like digital video, students would most likely have copyright claims in the works, even though they are created for the professors' use in class.

For instance, a student might create a special series of slides based on self-created photographs of animal or plant life to use for illustrative purposes in biology classrooms. Without a specific structure of work for hire or licensing, the student's professor would not be able to use those materials unless she or he received specific permission from the student, the copyright holder. Or a student might create a manual for operating an overhead projector that is used in a university classroom. The institution should acquire a license to use the manual before making copies and distributing them as a means to help instructors more efficiently use the machine.

As noted above, the courts have supported professors' claims in their class notes, and students would likely be supported for the same claim. If, however, a professor or university could substantiate a work-for-hire claim in the specific product created to support the professor's teaching, copyright control would go to the university, not the professor. Professors could claim copyright control under work for hire if they could show that they, rather than their universities, were the students' employers and that their students created works for them specifically within the scope of their duties as employees.

TEACH Act

When graduate students teach independently from their professors and control their own classrooms, they could retain a copyright in the materials they create for class, in the same way that their professors could. And they would also have the same responsibilities to make legal use of course materials and undergraduate students' works, consistent with personal and fair use, described in more detail in the third chapter. Teaching assistants are also bound by the same restrictions as their professors in the Technology, Education, and Copyright Harmonization Act, the TEACH Act. This act created new requirements for distance education, most involving direction of university administrative offices in education and technology, but those who teach in such courses are best prepared if they understand the act's requirements.

Often, teaching assistants whose interests move toward nontraditional teaching as a result of their own learning experiences in computer-enhanced classrooms opt to teach in online or distance courses, so knowledge of the TEACH Act could be particularly helpful to them. Computer-based courses in on-campus settings may involve use of online materials and entail digital interchange between or among participants in other classroom locations, and the TEACH Act applies to instruction in distance courses in nonprofit, accredited educational institutions as part of a teaching system that is mediated by an instructor. The TEACH Act (from H.R. 2215) allows a wide range of use of digital materials both to copy and to store, but its requirements are relatively stringent.

The act allows an instructor to digitally transmit whole performance of nondramatic literary or musical work, such as poetry readings and music other than opera, musicals, or music videos. It also allows instructors to transmit portions of all kinds of work, including dramatic and musical works. And it allows transmission of any work in still images. Essentially, the TEACH Act reflects intention to provide, in a digital classroom, the same kinds of teaching displays that would have been allowed in a face-to-face venue. That the work has to be digitally transmitted to do so requires limitations to inhibit misuse, however, and the TEACH Act provides explicit requirements in conjunction with its permissions. The institution supporting the distance course must have copyright policies in place and must provide copyright information and notice to students that the materials used in the course may be protected by copyright. In addition, the course materials transmitted by digital means must be provided only to students who are enrolled in the course. The institutions' information technology officials are responsible for limiting access to students enrolled in distance courses, for storing and disseminating the course content (as well as limiting its storage time), and for enforcing technological measures to manage the course materials. Student instructors who teach in distance classes must not only be aware of the parameters provided but also work in conjunction with university technology offices to comply with regulations in the TEACH Act, because their professors, who may not have taught in online or distance venues, may not be aware of the need. (See Copyright Management Center's distance education site for detailed information.)

To Collaborate or Not? Students' Choices

Clearly, students gain educational advantages from collaborating with their professors, other students, and administrators as a part of their academic experience. And in many classes, particularly in technical communication, collaborative assignments are part of the de rigueur structure. But, as issues discussed above make apparent, both students and their professors will be well served by understanding the potential impact of the choices they make. When all parties to collaborative interactions are aware of the legal implications of their choices and make decisions that are consistent with the outcomes they desire, collaborative work can be beneficial for all. Thus it is helpful for collaborative parties to educate themselves about the legal issues that will affect them and make clear agreements reflecting expectations for how their work will be treated before entering into joint projects.

However unreasonable it would be to undergo lengthy contract arrangements for every aspect of creative production within educational settings, it could be extremely beneficial to carefully consider negotiation processes in some cases. The classic classroom setting, where students produce hard copy research papers, provide essay exam responses, or develop creative prose or poetry as a means of learning the processes of creative communication, should require no contract for work that is used within the educational context. But where a student creates a particularly insightful creative work, the professor should be inhibited from reproducing it for use outside the classroom. Or when a student uses three-dimensional modeling to create a condominium unit for the virtual world Second Life, the professor should not attempt to claim it for future use or for sale (where virtual housing can cost, in real U.S. currency, ninety-five dollars per unit and higher).

Where educational endeavors today can lead to student production of work that has monetary value in or outside an educational setting, these issues become more important, and defining the intent for product use in conjunction with class development could be helpful for allaying problems that might result in the future. And as noted in the first chapter, students who work to develop patentable products should understand clearly the content of their contract with the university, should recognize how their authorship in the patent application will be treated, and should know the percentage of patent benefit that they will be allocated. In activities within the university in which students do not expect to engage in contract work, such as classrooms, instructors could provide language within their syllabi or course descriptions, noting the ways that student work products would be used. And absent specific work contracts with the university that should indicate students' relationships to the institution as producers, when students and professors work together to develop products, they could create documents noting clearly their roles for creation and expectations for treating the final products. Short of a formal arrangement, at minimum, students and professors should discuss their intentions for creating products produced through shared development.

3

Intellectual Products within Educational Settings

The Constitution's intellectual property clause provides creators and inventors with a limited monopoly in their work in order to support the overall goal of advancing knowledge. And the initial time limitation on creators' control—fourteen years after an author's death—provided a public domain of information from which to educate, build new knowledge, and participate in democratic dialogue. Today that limitation is virtually nonexistent as a result of the passage of the Copyright Term Extension Act, which created a "limitation" of life of the author plus 70 years in the case of authorship by natural persons and the lesser of either 95 years after date of publication or 120 years from creation of the work for corporate authorship. Because most of us will not find works created within our own lifetimes accessible as public domain, public access to information is currently severely inhibited. But copyright control is also limited by First Amendment goals and personal rights provided in the Constitution and is reflected in the 1976 Copyright Act's fair use doctrine. So, even as new amendments to copyright law have imposed limitations on the public domain, the public retains means for supporting its use of copyrighted material as a base for a viable democratic system. Students have rights as users of intellectual products, as do all other citizens, but their interests in using intellectual work is heightened during their educational enterprise. The law provides more leeway for using copyrighted material in educational settings, because these uses support the overall constitutional goal of the intellectual property provision for advancing learning and making a knowledgeable society possible; and it is within educational settings where supported use is most pertinent.

Students use materials as a basis for gathering information in the learning process and as a means to support their own creative work. And they employ information as a means to strengthen opinions and to participate in dialogue in classes on campus, as well as in their communities and even in national venues. In particular, in technical communication and fields like it, students engage in research and inquiry in humanistic ways, attempting to understand the impact of political power and policy choice, the effect of rhetorical arrangement and structuring in communications that have societal impact, and the influence of visual rhetoric, particularly on those who may not be aware of it. Making use of others' works as a basis for the activity of critical inquiry is prized among students and professors in technical communication, as it is in other fields where inquiry is the basis of much scholarly effort. These efforts in critical inquiry form the bases for critical speaking; First Amendment rights and fair use work together to make free speech possible, and free speech, in turn, supports learning and a robust citizenry capable of making educated analyses and decisions that affect the future of the country. And democracy is possible only when its citizens can participate in it. The educational institution is one venue in which students prepare themselves for the responsibility of citizenry and where they can actively learn how to participate in democratic systems.

Users' Rights in Intellectual Property
Fair Use

The 1976 Copyright Act's section 107 regarding fair use outlines some of the areas in which the public can legally use copyrighted work:

Limitations on Exclusive Rights: Fair Use

Notwithstanding the provisions of section 106, the fair use of a copyrighted work, including such use by reproduction in copies or phonorecords or by any other means specified by that section, for purposes such as criticism, comment, news reporting, teaching (including multiple copies for classroom use), scholarship, or research, is not an infringement of copyright. In determining whether the use made of a work in any particular case is a fair use the factors to be considered shall include—

(1) the purpose and character of the use, including whether such use is of a commercial nature or is for nonprofit educational purposes;

(2) the nature of the work;

(3) the amount and substantiality of the portion used in relation to the copyrighted work as a whole; and

(4) the effect of the use upon the potential market for or value of the copyrighted work. (17 U.S.C. §107 [1978])

Three broad elements play out in determining whether a use is considered noninfringing: the kind of product created by the use, the kind of product used, and the effects on the product used. Fair use allows access to copyrighted work through an "affirmative defense," a legal mechanism that enables a user to admit to using a copyrighted work, but to excuse that use when it occurs within proper circumstances. Fair use applies to all users and not just students and instructors within educational settings, but the focus here is on student use, so discussion is constructed with this in mind. The fair use guidelines are not limiting endpoints for using copyrighted intellectual products but instead provide a framework to understand how public use of copyrighted material is constitutionally supported. Moreover, the guidelines in fair use can also give students a means for expanded use of copyrighted work without infringement within educational settings.

Educators are allowed to provide multiple copies of copyrighted materials for classroom use, although the TEACH Act, explained in the second chapter, limits how these materials should be used within online classroom settings. And well within the realm of activities on campuses, fair use provides that students can use copyrighted materials for the basis of research, scholarship, campus news reporting, and critical comment. Regardless of the law's provisions supporting use of copyrighted work, there is always potential for a claim of infringement against a particular use, even if a claim is not potentially supportable. Whether or not a use is legal must be determined by examining the total context of a situation, so there are no clear-cut statements in the law about what is and what is not fair use or constitutionally allowed use. Both users and copyright holders must make best judgments about how to proceed in treating copyrighted works. Some copyright holders are extremely and even notoriously aggressive in their claims against copyright users. The Disney Corporation threatened to sue three different day care centers in Florida for decorating their walls with Disney characters. Although the suit was settled, Disney extended its reputation for hard-hitting copyright protection, while the Hanna-Barbera Company stepped in to offer use of its own cartoon characters in place of the Disney characters, which were painted over ("Disney Finds"). And Ludlow Music, holder of copyright to the Woody Guthrie song "This Land Is Your Land," threatened a suit against Jib-Jab Media for its animated parody, whose content included protected political speech (Electronic Frontier Foundation). Although Ludlow backed down from the suit and Disney settled its own, these cases illustrate the potential for legal threats against copyright use, whether or not clear merit for a suit exists. Students and their instructors should be aware that constitutional promises of support for use and delineation of that support in fair use do not guarantee that students or instructors will never face claims against them. Using materials for personal or educational reasons, or for constitutionally supported purposes, requires careful consideration of all circumstances of use in light of the ways they support the law's intended goals. Students must consider uses of copyrighted materials on a scale from "likely to be legally allowable" to "unlikely to be legally allowable."

Students typically use copyrighted materials in traditional ways, including accessing copyrighted print materials in books or articles, white papers, reports, maps, conference proceedings, mathematical problems, newspapers, architectural plans, photographs, artwork, films, musical scores and recordings, choreography, and scientific experimental procedures. And in particular, technical communication students also access digital products in the form of computer code, Weblogs, digital games, art, sounds, graphics, multiple forms of software music mp3's, and digital video, among others. Some materials that students might use are, by their nature, in the public domain and unprotected by copyright, so students can use them with little potential for legal threat. Uncopyrighted materials include facts of any kind; government documents; titles and short phrases; formerly copyrighted work that is now in the public domain, such as Shakespeare's writing; and works that are not fixed, such as choreography that has not been performed or recorded in some way.

Works that are copyrighted are still available for use, but such use must be considered with greater care, and whether students can use copyrighted materials without infringement hinges less on the forms of the products themselves than on the purposes, means, and extent of students' product use, as well as the venues in which students use them. When students copy pages from books to use as a base of work in class papers, there is little question that the use is supported both by rights in personal use and fair use, and by use of materials in the pursuit of educational purposes. Students might also copy whole articles in developing work for classes, and it would be highly unlikely that this use would be challenged. But if a student copied a whole book with the intention of selling it for profit, the student's use would likely be considered infringing. Regardless of their status as students or their location within an educational system, student infringement is subject to broader limitations imposed on noneducational uses if their activities allow them to benefit from other creators' work without valid licensing in commercial enterprises.

Students may also be able to legally use copyrighted materials in the future, because of a proposed law, the Orphan Works Act of 2008. The bill supporting this act, at this writing, is currently under consideration. It defines an orphan work as a copyrighted work whose author cannot be located after a "reasonably diligent search." Essentially, orphan works are considered "lost works" in that they could be unreasonably inaccessible for use. If this bill is passed, students would also have access to orphan works.

Even outside a situation involving an orphan work, existing law states explicitly that using copyrighted materials for criticism, comment, news reporting, teaching, scholarship, and research is allowed under fair use. And the basis for these allowable uses is, in part, in their support of free speech, discussed in detail in this chapter. The ways in which copyrighted materials can be used without infringement are clarified below.

Criticism

Because criticism forms the basis for democratic dialogue, it is supported by a copyright law that allows users to employ and copy the information that is the object of criticism. A current example of critical commentary that would likely be supported by fair use is one in which syndicated columnist Michelle Malkin posted clips from musician Akon's rhythm and blues video on YouTube, accompanied by her criticism decrying his misogynistic lyrics and actions as "vulgar and degrading" ("Fair Use Fight"). Although currently this case has not yet been treated in the law, Malkin's use of Universal Music Group's Akon video would likely be allowed under fair use because she employed the copy as a basis for critical commentary.

That fair use supports criticism is particularly helpful in academic settings, because critical thinking forms the base of much of the work that students and their professors undertake in educational enterprises. In fact, the best learning situations require that students think critically so that they can understand the world around them through a process of questioning rather than absorbing memorized, rote information.

Comment

At times, users of copyrighted materials may reflect an author's intention not to criticize but only to comment on a copyrighted work. Supported by fair use, commentary allows society's free flow of ideas, particularly in educational settings, where users can comment on a work to help students understand it. Fair use also supports the use of copyrighted work as a means of explanation for movie reviews, text commentaries, and art criticism, among other purposes.

Online commentary proliferates in Weblogs (blogs), where the originator of the blog provides primary commentary but solicits responses from the public. Both the originator's and the respondents' opinions can appear in the form of commentary and can be validly supported by fair use.

News Reporting

A free press is central to a well-operating democracy, so the Framers made sure to safeguard legal means to support it. Fair use reflects this intention by allowing noninfringing uses of copyrighted material in news reporting. Fair use for news reporting is rarely challenged, but the court in *Byrne v. BBC* notes,

> Not all unlicensed uses of copyrighted material for inclusion in broadcasts that present material of interest to the public are protected by the fair use doctrine, even if they are labeled "news reporting" by defendants. If the purpose of the use was to entertain, rather than inform, see *Schumann v. Albuquerque Corp.*, 664 F. Supp. 473, 477 (D.N.M. 1987), or if equally informative non-infringing alternatives were available, see *Roy Export Co. v. Columbia Broad. Sys., Inc.*, 503 F. Supp. 1137, 1144 (S.D.N.Y. 1980), then the first fair use factor tips in favor of the plaintiff. Cf. Los Angeles News Serv., 149 F.3d at 994 (copying of news footage for redistribution to overseas news organizations was not fair use). (234)

When the use is actually intended to report the news so that the public is apprised of events that affect it, fair use of copyrighted materials for news reporting is supported. Student newspapers and blogs may validly use copyrighted materials to report news. And students will also find that fair use of copyrighted works extends to news reporting in online venues.

Teaching

It makes perfect sense that the overall constitutional goal of advancing society's knowledge would be reflected in the fair use doctrine, so it is no surprise that fair use supports use of copyrighted materials for teaching. Supporting the educational enterprise in this way affects both institutions and student populations as a whole. Where students need access to information in multiple forms as a basis for reading, research, and commentary, their professors need the same, to understand issues that affect society in broader and deeper terms but also to aid students in learning. In particular, graduate students who work in their universities as teaching assistants may draw on fair use, using copyrighted teaching materials in their own classes; but access for teaching purposes extends to students in other circumstances as well. Students may be asked to prepare materials for oral presentation in class settings and would most likely be protected in their use of copyrighted materials for this purpose. They might also prepare materials to use for education within social, political, or religious organizations on campus, and their use of copyrighted materials within this framework would most likely be supported. Of course, most directly, instructors benefit students by using rights in fair use to support student learning. And they should remain aware that teaching in virtual classrooms is now treated differently in instances where educational activities are targeted by the TEACH Act, noted above.

Scholarship

Scholarly work is dependent on use of copyrighted materials, and scholarly activity, by its nature, encompasses criticism, commentary, and educational purposes based in part on the extension of free speech. Without access to others' intellectual products for scholarly purposes, there would be no academic examination or exploration, learning would be inhibited, and the constitutional goals within the intellectual property clause, as well as the overriding goals of the Constitution, would be thwarted.

The Digital Age

Although the legal basis for fair use has not changed as a result of widespread digitization of information, the more malleable nature of digital products, in contrast to hard copy works, makes them easier to access, copy, and disseminate. The result has been a reactive response to tighten access to digitized intellectual products and to inhibit the kinds of use, copy, and dissemination that fair use has supported for hard copy work. Regardless, the conceptual basis and policy behind fair use are still alive, even in the digital age, and students' rights to the same kind of access that would have been supported when information existed only in hard copy format must still be respected today. (Digitization and its effects are discussed in more detail in the last two chapters.)

Guidelines for Use

Even though the law clearly lays out a basis for supporting use of copyrighted works, fair use also guides users in employing materials while still ensuring that copyright holders' intellectual products are not misused. These guidelines help to define the contextual parameters for how users employ intellectual products while refraining from infringing them. The structure of fair use provides the categories of characterization below as a basis for examining whether a use has gone so far that it is no longer considered noninfringing.

Amount and Substantiality

Fair use dictates that a user should consider whether the amount of the work used is a substantial or minimal portion of the work. If a user copies an extensive amount of a work, the use is less likely to be legitimate. But what is considered extensive depends on the work itself. Intellectual property "legend" holds that copying twenty-five words is always allowable, but if the work is a haiku, then the whole work would be copied and the amount would clearly be so substantial that the extreme amount of copying could infringe the work. A Supreme Court case, *Harper and Row Publishers, Inc. v. Nation Enterprises* illustrates that whether an amount is substantial turns less on the actual amount than the importance of the particular text copied. Former president Gerald Ford had written his autobiography and licensed the work to Harper and Row. When the *Nation* magazine published less than four hundred words of the text in its journal, the Supreme Court found it to be a copyright infringement. Despite the relative minimal number of words within a book of several hundred pages, the Court found that copying this particular text was so important to the work, so substantial, that fair use failed as a defense.

In contrast, in *Kelly v. Arriba Soft Corporation*, the Ninth Circuit Court ruled in favor of the defendant, who had copied a photographer's photos to make thumbnails of them for its search engine. The court determined that Arriba Soft's use was "transformative," which supports a fair use finding. Transformative use is upheld when a court finds that the user changed the original work to such an extent that it repurposes or "transforms" it so that it is no longer a copy of an original. Creating a transformative use is distinguished from creating a "derivative work," which would be considered a violation of copyright.

In *Bill Graham Archives v. Dorling Kindersley, Ltd.*, the court declared the defendant's use of full images of Grateful Dead posters a transformative fair use. In this case the defendant had used the images as a basis for explaining the historical journey of the Grateful Dead rock band in a biographical documentation. The court noted that the use was transformative because the images, as presented in the biography, could not have been substituted for the original posters, the forms from which they were copied. The use of the reduced-size images in the biography was to explain the nature of the band and enhance understanding of the biographical text.Not all works based on original copyrighted work are transformative in nature. For instance, a derivative work is one that reflects the original copyrighted product to the extent that it extends the substance of the work. The film *West Side Story* is a derivative work of *Romeo and Juliet*, and *My Fair Lady* is a derivative work of *Pygmalion.* Creating derivative works is not supported by fair use, because a derivative work is so closely based on the originally copyrighted work that making a derivation would use the essence of the original. Note that although parodies might seem like derivative works, by their nature they are transformative and are completely new creative products. More important, parodies (of both trademarked and copyrighted works) are also a form of speech, protected by the First Amendment, as well as fair use. Parodies are discussed in more detail later in this chapter.

Nature of the Work

Another aspect of fair use that must be considered in employing copyrighted work is the nature of the work that is being copied. If the intellectual product is of particular importance to the public and copying it would affect the public interest in an important way, use is more likely to be noninfringing. For example, the district court held that *Time* magazine could not prevent fair use of still frames of the Zapruder film in which President Kennedy's assassination was recorded because the tape was of great public value (*Time, Inc. v. Bernard Geis Associates*). Works based on facts are more likely to be accessible through fair use, whereas imaginative works are less likely to be usable without infringement. For instance, students may wish to use historical documents in their work and would likely be supported as long as the work is cited, not copied wholesale, and used as a basis for scholarly discussion, comparison, criticism, or commentary. But a student's use of the whole of a copyrighted contemporary music file, especially for the purpose of entertainment, would most likely be considered an infringing use.

Purpose and Character

In addition to other considerations, the kind of use a student (or professor or other user) makes is an important element for examination. If the purpose is to educate, to criticize, to form the base of political speech, then the use is more likely to be allowed. This aspect of fair use reflects very specific aspects of the constitutional intellectual property clause by focusing directly on public benefit that follows from using copyrighted work. If the purpose of copying a work is only to create an economic benefit for the user, then this aspect of fair use would not be satisfied. In the case where students copy materials to support their learning processes, fair use is more likely to be supported, because students most often use and create work within educational settings as a part of their educational process and the products they create usually have little economic value. However, particularly graduate students with extensive training, but also undergraduate students, do have potential to build valuable products that could be marketed for profit either during their educational careers or afterward. The special circumstances in which they are allowed more leeway to use copyrighted products for school efforts would not extend to other circumstances under fair use.

So when a student uses copyrighted images on a Web site as a basis for critical exploration of those images and their meaning in or effect on society, particularly if the use is within technical communication classes in educational settings, the purpose of criticism as a means to advance learning would allow leeway for support in fair use. But if a student instead used the same images only to decorate a Web site, even for a class assignment, the use would be more likely to be considered infringing.

Effect on Marketability

To protect creators' interests in their work, fair use includes a requirement that the copyrighted work's marketability not be harmed by a user who might make a copy of the original and gain financially in the creator's stead. This portion of the doctrine is not intended to inhibit the kind of criticism that might affect marketability; it is also not in place to disallow parodies. But if a user copies so much of a copyrighted work or distributes it in a way that overcomes the copyright holder's benefits in distribution so that it is devalued for potential buyers or licensees, fair use will not prevent a court from finding infringement and disallowing fair use. In the classic case *Sony Corp of America v. Universal City Studios, Inc.*, usually referred to as "Betamax," the Supreme Court supported a personal use right for an individual to videotape a whole television program for future viewing. The Court focused on the rights of individuals to make home copies for personal use and noted that individuals' personal use copying would not affect the market value of the copied product. Students might copy paragraphs of a book to use as a basis for critical comment in a class paper, with little potential for violation.

Fair Use of Student Work

Just as others' work can be used by students, students' and professors' works can be accessible through fair use by others or by each other. For example, a technical communication student might create a blog that, in part, examines critical concepts in technical communication, such as analysis of visual rhetoric in welcome screens touting new digital products. An instructor may be supported by fair use if he or she copies a portion of the blog to use in class as a basis for teaching commentary. Or the instructor might quote from the blog in a published paper as a way to support or illustrate a statement about student commentary in technical communication. So, if we assume the amount and substantiality of the portion of the work used by the instructor are not so extreme as to usurp the student's work, because the usage was for critical commentary or illustration, it was not likely to affect marketability of a student's work and, in this case, because it was for educational purposes, the potential for support by fair use is high.

By the same token, students may also make fair uses of their professors' work. In addition to using published articles as a basis for research and analyses in their own critical analytical projects, students may also use portions of class handouts, quoting guidelines for assignments, for example, to develop their own responses for class. And students might later refer to guidelines from course handouts in work they produce outside class, as long as the work is properly attributed, does not amount to such a substantial use that it appropriates the professor's work, does not affect the marketability of the professor's work, and is a basis for critical commentary, news reporting, analysis, or educational purpose.

Even though greater leeway is provided for copying and use in educational settings, instructors should teach students about copying as if they were using materials outside the educational institution. This way, they would be prepared for dealing with materials after they leave the academy.

Students' Free Speech Rights

Students also have rights to use protected intellectual products based on the Constitution's First Amendment grant of free speech safeguards. Likewise, students' work can be subject to free speech expressions of others. The Supreme Court has a consistent history of supporting parodies as protected speech, both in copyrighted items and in trademarked work. Representative of the inviolate nature of the First Amendment is the case of Chilean political activists Ariel Dorfman and Armand Mattelart, who were able to fend off Disney's claims of infringement through their parody of Scrooge McDuck and his nephews, Huey, Dewey, and Louie, in *How to Read Donald Duck*. In their parodic complaint against what they saw as Disney's imperialist propaganda in its comics imported into Chile, the authors re-created Disney's comic characters acting out a capitalist agenda. The nature of the parody, as political speech, led to a decision that it would be protected and that Disney would not prevail in a suit on copyright infringement. More recent Supreme Court cases also support free speech in parody. In *Campbell v. Acuff-Rose Music*, the Court upheld 2 Live Crew's right to parody Roy Orbison's "Oh Pretty Woman." The Court found that 2 Live Crew's lyrics characterizing the song's object as a "big, hairy woman," a "baldheaded woman," and a "two-timin' woman" created such a contrast to the Orbison version that it made a statement about the contrast between characterizations of white and black society and should be protected speech.

Supreme Court cases indicate a continuing pattern of support for parody as free speech in fair use as well. In *Leibovitz v. Paramount Pictures Inc.*, photographer Annie Leibovitz sued Paramount for its parody of her famous photo of a pregnant actress, Demi Moore, which was published in an issue of *Vanity Fair* magazine. Paramount advertised its movie *Naked Gun 33⅓: The Final Insult* with a parody of the Leibovitz photo that superimposed the head of the movie's star, Leslie Nielson, over the head of the actress so his head was depicted on the pregnant body of Demi Moore. The photo was accompanied by a caption that read "Due this month." The Court held that even though the parody was used for commercial purposes, it was still protected fair use that has no substantial effect on marketability of the original. The statement in the case regarding the Court's focus is significant:

> In focusing the first factor inquiry upon the "transformative" nature of the use, the Court explicitly abandoned the statement in *Sony Corp. of America v. Universal City Studios, Inc.*, . . . that "every commercial use of copyrighted material is presumptively . . . unfair," *id.* at 451. *See Campbell*, 510 U.S. at 583–85. Instead, the Court recalled its statement in *Harper & Row, Publishers, Inc. v. Nation Enterprises* . . . that commercial use is only "'a separate factor that tends to weigh against a finding of fair use.'" *Campbell*, 510 U.S. at 585 (quoting *Harper & Row*, 471 U.S. 585. at 562). (9)

In more recent cases, the Supreme Court let the district courts' decisions stand in favor of fair use and free speech interests either by affirming the courts' decisions or by refusing to review them (denying certiorari). *Mattel, Inc. v. MCA Records, Inc.* concerns the Danish rock band Aqua's use of Mattel's Barbie trademark in its popular song "Barbie Girl." The band's video and song portray the Barbie character singing lines such as "I'm a blonde bimbo girl, in a fantasy world" in a high-pitched voice, while the Ken character entices her to "go party." After the song and video reached the top forty song chart, Mattel sued the band's music distributor, MCA, for trademark infringement. The Supreme Court upheld the district court's finding that Aqua's parody was not likely to create confusion that would lead consumers to believe that Mattel produced the song, and that its parody is supported by the First Amendment. The Court's discussion of this case noted that the Barbie character carries a kind of iconic expression that society has assimilated as part of its cultural understanding. The Court explained that a trademark tied to a commercial interest is not enough to override the free speech support for cultural expression by allowing use of the mark for parody.

In *Hustler Magazine, Inc. v. Falwell*, the Supreme Court upheld *Hustler*'s First Amendment right to parody the well-known preacher Jerry Falwell as a public figure. The magazine's parody depicted Falwell telling the history of his "first time" in a drunken state with his mother in an outhouse. Despite the inflammatory nature of the parody, and independent of an assessment of bad taste, the Supreme Court declared that, by its nature, the parody was not attempting to depict actual facts but lampooned Falwell because he was a potential parody subject as a public figure.

Parodies of trademarks are allowable by way of First Amendment argument rather than fair use, although both have a connection to or basis in free speech. Fair use applies to work that is copyrighted, based on its support of parody embodied in the four factors of fair use within the copyright act, explained above. But copyrighted parodies may also be protected through the First Amendment. Courts may conflate fair use and First Amendment treatment of their case subjects because the reasoning behind the constitutional provisions supporting free speech is common to both fair use and First Amendment issues. Strictly speaking, fair use applies not to trademarks but to copyrighted work alone. But First Amendment support of free speech applies to both.

Rosemary Coombe has examined in extensive detail the cultural appropriation of meaning from commercial trademarks and copyrighted works. She discusses ways that users respond to, interact with, parody, comment on, and sometimes appropriate common representations of objects within our culture, all as a means to interact within the culture that these symbols represent. She makes a broad use of examples of commercial images and concepts that have assumed greater meaning within the culture than what their creators initially intended. She notes, for instance, that Mr. Clean, Lucky Charms, and Geritol, among other brands, have been "recoded" to carry more meaning than was their initial intent (57), so characterization of an older group of Americans as "the Geritol Generation," for example, creates new meaning while simultaneously maintaining its original brand identification. Students may find brand references enticing as a base for commentary, as in those common symbols worn on students' t-shirts, such as "Cocaine-Cola" and multiple parodies of the dairy industry's "Got Milk?" campaign, with shirts or bumper stickers displaying "Got Ripped Off?" "Got Beer?" "Got Muscle?" "Got Jesus?" Got Gas?" among others.

Where these kinds of parodies may merely seem amusing, students might also use parody and other forms of label "recoding" as a basis for serious commentary. A student who parodies the "Be all you can be" slogan for army recruitment by accompanying it with images of gravestones would be making critical comment regarding the futility of war, and another who juxtaposes the Beatles song "All You Need Is Love" with images of Hitler paired with Osama bin Laden would be criticizing those who find no need to go to war.

For students, what may be the most important aspect of First Amendment protection of parody is that it makes available a form of criticism that is effective and often enticing as a tool for engaging in critical thinking about the objects of parodies. Materials like these, that enhance the learning experience, are invaluable, and the law ensures that these kinds of criticism are available. In addition, students may also find parodies and other First Amendment uses of materials a helpful way to express their own ideas and to form a basis for reflection on topics with which they might not otherwise engage. They may also participate in heightened responses to criticism when their own work is used by those who make supported free expressions. Students then truly interact within a dialogic process of learning that is enabled and supported by free speech.

It is also helpful for students to realize the national importance of free speech as a foundation for our country. While new intellectual property laws consistently limit rights of access, free speech is nevertheless upheld as an important element of law to be abided by. Even as other means of access to copyrighted work have diminished, courts have consistently upheld use of parodies on the basis of their nature as cultural criticism and commentary. This kind of support is significant for students in the throes of educational enterprise, as they build their perceptions of what it means to be a part of a national political system based on democratic principles.

Digital Millennium Copyright Act

With a grant of rights of access come limits on and responsibility for personal and educational uses. Students who have begun their educational careers after the passage of the Digital Millennium Copyright Act (DMCA) will find that their rights are more limited than those of students who came before them. The DMCA was developed to prevent users of digital products, primarily in the forms of CDs and DVDs, from creating or using technology to circumvent protection devices that were put in place to prevent copying. The DMCA's supporters forwarded the law because of fears that digital products could be easily copied and disseminated in pristine form, undetectable as copies, unlike their predecessors, videotapes, which degrade in copied form. The Recording Industry Association of America (RIAA) and the Motion Picture Association of America (MPAA), among others, claimed that users would take advantage of the digital copying technology to such an extent that they would destroy the music, movie, and software industries. And to further encourage a law that would protect digital products, they asserted that the United States should harmonize its law with Europe. European members of the World Intellectual Property Organization wished to ensure that users worldwide would be halted from copying and disseminating digital work (Sharp 27–39; McCormick 711). Under the DMCA, anyone who *creates* a device that allows the user to circumvent its antiprivacy tools built into the intellectual product would be liable for criminal conduct, and anyone who *uses* a device to do the same would also be criminally liable.

The DMCA also makes it a criminal offense to manufacture, sell, or distribute code-cracking devices used for decrypting digital protections in intellectual products. This means that students who find means, such as "work-arounds," to copy DVDs or CDs by manipulating computer code could be criminally liable for their conduct. It also means that if a student receives e-mail describing a means to circumvent a encryption device and forwards it to someone else to question it, to comment on it, or for any other purpose, he or she could also be held criminally liable under the DMCA.

The DMCA has been widely criticized for its hindrance of fair use and its inhibition of learning. Despite its explicit language stating, "Nothing in this section shall affect rights, remedies, limitations, or defenses to copyright infringement, including fair use, under this title" (§ 1201, Circumvention of Copyright Protection Systems), the DMCA is limiting to students and their professors, whose educational enterprise relies on access to research materials in digital form, just as it relied on the same in hard copy form when digitization was not the base of information transfer. Regardless of its claims to the contrary, the DMCA makes fair use ineffectual by creating criminal penalties for accessing material that could be usable under fair use. Without access there could be no use at all, either supported by fair use or not. So fair use is nullified by the DMCA, or as one author put it, "while it remains legal under the DMCA to make fair use of a lawfully accessed work, there probably will be no device available that is legally capable of making the copy" (Sharp 35). The DMCA's suppression of fair use is harmful to all students because it hampers their ability to learn. But particularly for computing students, who rely on reverse engineering and decoding to discover means to create new coded products or alleviate problems in code that operates poorly, the inhibition on learning about encryption systems through working with their code is academically stifling.

In a move to acknowledge the need for access and to provide greater support for educational endeavors, the Library of Congress's Copyright Office passed a new law exempting for three years, among six classes of use, security code circumvention for audiovisual works when it is "for educational use in the classroom by media studies or film professors." But even though this exemption helps to support educational access for a limited time, other aspects of the DMCA are extensively prohibitive, even in educational settings.

Penn State University law professor Jeff Sharp, in his extensive treatment of this issue, points out that the greatest impact of the DMCA is its negative influence on educational progress (2). He notes that, among other detriments, "First, public domain material may someday be locked up through technological barriers requiring payments for access. Second, the ability to except legally accessed content for fair use presentation in the classroom may be severely degraded or eliminated through the application of technological barriers" (Sharp 42). As Sharp points out, the fair use exemptions for education that provide access to hard copy documents are defeated when educational material is reified in code. And, he asserts, "Congress knew that fair use, as it had been articulated judicially numerous times, was being written out of the law" as to digital content (Sharp 51). He believes that today, "digital copyrights trump fair use" (Sharp 77). Not only does the DMCA's potential application limit students' access to information, but such access would otherwise be available had the DMCA not been enacted. Today, teaching depends on digitally developed materials in the same way that it depended on hard copy in the past. To hinder access to the material that is the base for learning in the digital age is to destroy a publicly accessible educational process.

The DMCA does provide exemptions from its reach in favor of nonprofit libraries, archives, and in limited ways, educational institutions. It also limits Internet service providers (ISPs) from criminal liability for the acts of its users as "safe harbors" as long as ISPs are unaware of infringing activity or immediately stop service to infringers once they do become aware. And universities' status as safe harbors under the DMCA is supported in a special report in distance education in the digital realm, provided by the Copyright Office. It notes that section 512 is in place to protect universities as providers of online education (U.S. Copyright Office). Nevertheless, as a result of the DMCA, today universities are inhibited in the kind of access they can provide to students to support their learning activities both in and out of classrooms. And, as noted above, some of this access is further limited by the TEACH Act.

Despite the DMCA's exemption for encryption research, Edward Felten, a computing professor at Princeton University, was attacked by the Secure Digital Music Initiative (SDMI) after he and his students successfully met its challenge to decrypt its software for a prize of ten thousand dollars. Felten responded to the challenge as a means to encourage his students to learn about encryption devices, and when he and his students were successful in decrypting the code, they prepared to present their findings at USENIX, an academic conference on computing. In an ultimate irony, after learning that Felten and his students were successful, SDMI threatened criminal action against Felten and demanded that he and his students refrain from their plans to present the data, using the DMCA as their weapon. Felten filed a plea in federal court asking the court to declare that he and his students could rightfully present their findings at the conference and in article form. He eventually withdrew the plea after the federal government and the RIAA assured him that threats would not be repeated against his digital research (EFF "Felten," Aug. 7, 2002). Unfortunately, not every professor or student has been given those reassurances, and the threat that inhibits research still exists in the DMCA.

In a well-known case, the MPAA applied aggressive use of DMCA reach across national borders to persuade the Norwegian government to arrest a sixteen-year-old boy and his father (who owned a Web site where his son's materials were posted) and confiscate the boy's computer, based on the belief that he had developed the "DeCSS," a piece of code that was able to defeat the Content Scrambling System (CSS) encryption in DVD technology. Social rather than legal response seemed to override the effectiveness of DMCA limitations when members of the hacker community countered what they considered a broad reach by the MPAA. On the basis of arguments in support of fair use and the First Amendment, they posted the DeCSS code on multiple Web sites, printed it on T-shirts and ties, and made it available through multiple means of wide distribution. In an interesting twist, where the DMCA, if followed to the letter of the law, had been successfully applied in this case, education, intellectual invention, and new knowledge development would have been inhibited, but the *attempt* to apply the DMCA created a backlash that actually encouraged innovation in its political dissent. The "Gallery of CSS Descramblers" is a testament to the inventive responses. It includes the original source code for the DeCSS descrambler but also includes a new version of DeCSS, the "tiniest known C implementation" at only 434 bytes; a mathematical description of the DeCSS algorithm; Java characters that explain the DeCSS code; and a DeCSS haiku that is "both a commentary on the DeCSS situation and a correct and complete description of the descrambling algorithm" (Touretzky).

Both students and their professors should be aware of the prospective problems they could face with possible violation of the DMCA. But the broad backlash against the constraints on fair use and the potential for education based on digital media are encouraging political action. At this writing, Congressman Richard Boucher is leading a charge to overcome the ill effects of the DMCA by sponsoring a new congressional bill, the Digital Media Consumers' Rights Act (DMCRA). This new bill would reaffirm fair use and clearly establish the "Betamax" standard, which provides legal support for individual personal copying of copyrighted material. It would also require proper labeling of CDs and DVDs so that consumers would know whether the media is encrypted with anticircumvention code. Until this bill is passed or the courts reverse the previous direction of their holdings, students should be attentive to their uses of encrypted media.

Peer-to-Peer File Sharing

The words *students* and *intellectual property* usually come together in discussions regarding peer-to-peer (P2P) file sharing and the recent cases involving Napster, Grokster, and Aimster that treat music file sharing and potential copyright violation. In a congressional hearing by the 21st Century Competitiveness Subcommittee of the House Education and Workforce Committee, Dan Glick, CEO of the MPAA, asserted,

> Piracy is the greatest obstacle the film industry currently faces. A recently released study, conducted by the international consulting firm LEK, found that U.S. film industry lost $6.1 billion to piracy in 2005. That same study estimated that 44% of our industry's domestic

losses, over $500 million annually, are attributable to college students. An earlier Deloitte and Touche study estimated that approximately 400,000 films are illegally downloaded every day. CacheLogic, an Internet monitoring group, has estimated that over 60 percent of all Internet traffic in the U.S. is attributable to peer-to-peer usage. Furthermore, well over 90 percent of all the content on P2P networks consists of unauthorized copyrighted files. ("Combating Internet Piracy")

Despite the RIAA's filings of more than 1,062 copyright infringement suits at 132 colleges and universities between 2003 and 2006 (McCormick 713), none of these defendants has been found guilty ("Ohio U Failing Students in RIAA Attack"). Because of the nature of P2P file sharing, accounting for which and how many students participate in potentially infringing use of copyrighted materials is difficult, if not impossible, to note exactly. Regardless of the exact numbers of abuses on P2P networks, most would concede that students on college campuses are in the highest range of those who might be. With the numbers and concession to the realization of how widely college students populate P2P networks comes a blanket assumption of copyright infringement in individual cases, whether warranted or not. (See Logie for extensive treatment.)

When students use others' copyrighted work without a license or without valid personal or fair use exemption, their uses are infringing, and on both legal and ethical bases, they should refrain from these kinds of uses. But P2P networks can also be employed for a myriad of noninfringing uses. The P2P structure allows individuals who are digitally connected to each other to transfer materials back and forth on a one-to-one basis. This kind of file transfer is different from that which allows individuals to access a common database holding digital materials that can be uploaded to the individual user. The P2P structure, in itself, is not violative of legal limitations, but the way it is used instead determines whether there is a violation. Students can validly make their own work available through P2P structures, and they may also access public domain materials through P2Ps without infringing the work. In addition, they may also access files that are licensed for download within P2P structures.

There are a number of advantages to P2P structures: participants may possess files that are not commonly found on databases or they may place their own digital files within reach; the P2P structure is inexpensive because it requires little server space to make information available to a broad spectrum of users, whereas a database would have to house thousands of different files to accommodate all users who might need or wish to access the information; and because P2P structures are distributed across a broad network of users, they are less vulnerable to total system breakdown or to attack, unlike the potential from a single database structure that could fall if its server failed. These advantages can be helpful in university settings where students are aided by networking bases that allow them to share class notes, post portions of collaborative projects, and transfer bibliographic material to each other. Although absolute determination of infringement would depend on contextual treatment of each individual instance of use, these uses are generally noninfringing. Students could also transfer public domain materials without infringement and transfer materials to which they have licenses without copyright violation. And within the realm of fair use or free speech, noted above, students could also legally transfer digital information. Wholesale condemnation of the structure itself serves no purpose other than to limit the potential benefits of a technological advancement in information transfer.

Conflicts develop, however, in cases where copyright holders claim license violations. These conflicts have been dealt with in the courts in several recent cases, and the courts' instructions, although not focused specifically on educational use, have proved to favor copyright holders. By far the most publicized case is *A&M Records, Inc. v. Napster, Inc.*, in which a student, Shawn Fanning, created a P2P software application so he could share digital files with his friends. After Napster became a private company and made its software available for free, it became extremely popular among college students around the country because it allowed them to share music files converted to mp3 format and, later, digital movie files. Its popularity was broad enough to attract the attention of musicians, songwriters, and the recording and film industries, who saw the P2P structure as a threat to their copyright holdings and potential profits. The Ninth Circuit Court affirmed the district court's finding that Napster's claim of fair use was not validly supported by law, in part as a result of Napster's direct financial benefit gained and because it could have supervised its users' infringing conduct and did not. Students in technical communication, digital media, computational media, and similar fields will find the courts' opinions instructive, especially when they develop digital products in the forms of instructional materials, games, or other forms of digital products that allow or encourage individuals to interact and share coded objects as a part of their interaction within the digital space. Understanding the fine distinctions in these cases can be informative for those who intend to build digital worlds or access points that encourage users' independent action.

After the Napster case, the courts dealt with two different legal aspects in a similar P2P treatment in *Metro-Goldwyn-Mayer Studios, Inc. v. Grokster, Ltd.* (Axberg). The Grokster case also involved a P2P network. Unlike the Napster court, the Ninth Circuit ruled that Grokster could not be made legally liable for the infringements of its users and based its decision on the earlier Supreme Court ruling in the Betamax case that upheld the right of an individual to copy material for personal use on the basis of the network as a safe harbor. Without a ruling of this kind, devices like TiVo and iPods could be useless for the kind of personal choice that makes them popular. And students whose postgraduation goal is to build software to encourage user interaction could find that the creative potential of their products is severely limited.

The Supreme Court agreed to hear the case a year later, and significantly, even though the Court determined that Grokster had violated the DMCA on the basis of an "active inducement" theory of liability, it approached its decision with new legal reasoning that did not overturn the Betamax decision. The active inducement theory posits that the P2P network provider would be liable for its users' infringement if it promoted the network's ability to provide a means for infringement. The Court found that Grokster included on its Web site no tools to filter its data to diminish the potential for infringement and thus determined there was clear evidence that Grokster induced its users to infringe copyrights. By using this line of reasoning to find that Grokster would be held liable for its users' infringement, the Court left the safe harbor reasoning in Betamax intact. This reasoning is significant for universities, which could potentially protect themselves from liability for their students' infringements with the safe harbor argument.

Arguably, this concept of inducement, also sometimes called secondary infringement, may open the door for other kinds of liability claims against participants in educational endeavors. A university might require that all students use distributed learning software such as T-Square or CompClass for online learning. If it also required or suggested that students upload and share copies of copyrighted work without acquiring a license to do so, the university might be found liable on the basis of inducement. But as *Grokster* showed, to be liable for inducement, there has to be an infringement, the inducer has to have taken particular steps to ask specifically or to directly encourage a user to infringe, and the inducer has to have intended for the infringement to occur.

Under these requirements, if students illegally copy or distribute course-required expensive software or even expensive textbooks to avoid purchasing them for class, an instructor would not be liable for inducement unless he or she actively took steps to make illegal copying possible, encouraged students to make unlicensed copies, and intended that they do so. By the same token, if a student provided illegally downloaded materials in class and a professor displayed them, the professor might be found personally liable for copyright violation in displaying the work, but without satisfying the elements of inducement, a copyright holder would likely find it difficult to support an inducement claim.

Whenever use of another's work is in question, the user must consider his or her own responsibilities in treating available works. At times, that responsibility can be to use the work for supporting free speech or for educational purposes provided for through fair use. But in other cases, users must take responsibility for their actions and ensure that they make all efforts not to violate the legal and ethical rights of others.

4

Authorship, Plagiarism, and Copyright

Difficulty sometimes arises in rectifying the seemingly incongruous perceptions of students as vessels for taking in what their professors have to offer and of students as independent thinkers and new knowledge producers who build on what they learn in classes. And by the nature of their status as learners rather than the learned, students may also be considered unformed; or in the process of developing as creators. The irony, of course, is that even the most published of thinkers are always in the process of learning and adding to new knowledge, or they will no longer be publishable for lack of new contributions and new ideas.

For students to be perceived as authors, professors and administrators must view them as valid contributors to the general academic endeavor. Authorship, by the nature of many academics' construction of it, provides power in the individual who claims it, and it may be this hurdle of perception or misperception that allows instructors, administrators, and their institutions to overlook authorship in students' work. The enterprise of authorship in itself is not clear in its divisions between who is and who is not an author, or between who has power and authority in authorship and who does not. Shaun Slattery's research points to another area problematic to technical communicators. He notes that in workplace writing, which is created over distributed networks similar to many for which our students prepare, technical communicators' authorship is difficult to identify; technical communicators write in situations in which they have neither control over content nor the choice to generate work of original texts. Slack, Miller, and Doak also point to particular problems in determining authorship in products of technical communication, which are often derived through the demand of those who use technical communicators as a conduit for information. These authors make the case that technical communicators do create works of authorship and thus retain the power that accompanies it. But for those whose authorship is unclearly specified, especially as students, the ability to make claims of authorship can be limited.

To add to the difficulty, distinct differences between legal and literary-philosophical treatments of authorship may lead to confusion in assessing authorship in application. These two ways of thinking, legal and literary, construct authorship in different ways, attaching differing sources of power to each construction, ultimately affecting the outcome of societal application of those constructs in such a way that the resulting conclusions can create vastly different outcomes.

The following section explores what it means to be an author, from both a legal standpoint and a literary or societal one. Examining both these areas is important for delving into student authorship because students' creative works are assessed through both legal and literary structures, and the inconsistencies between the differing characterizations of authorship under the law and through the screen of literary thought can lead to significant misunderstandings or mistreatment of students' work. After establishing the differences in treatment of authorship, this chapter provides discussion of plagiarism and its role in relation to students. Then the last portion of the chapter focuses on plagiarism databases such as Turnitin.com and the legal and ethical ramifications of use of these kinds of sites in treating students' work. Because most intellectual products gain legal attributes in authorship under copyright law, the discussion here focuses on this area of the law exclusively.

Authorship

Peter Jaszi explains that literary and philosophical approaches to constructing "authorship" continue to muddle understanding of the law (Jaszi, "Toward a Theory" 455), despite the explicit explanations of authorship and its legal impact under the 1976 Copyright Act. He notes that authorship, as it was initially treated in the law, was conceived from eighteenth-century Romantic epistemological belief systems influenced by literary and artistic cultures (455). Under Romantic concepts of authorship, the author is imbued with an essence of superiority in the presumed potential to reach the transcendent. So the abstract value in his (or her, but in the eighteenth century, almost always his) reach—more accurately, *near* reach—to the transcendent created a sense of authority in knowledge.

Jaszi makes clear that authorship is "a culturally, politically, economically, and socially constructed category" of understanding rather than one that is real or natural (459). But with this concept of authorship comes the unwavering belief that it is a "distinct and privileged category of activity, that generates products of social value, entitling the practitioners (the 'authors') to unique rewards" (466). Authorship is not a real category but is constructed from belief systems that during the eighteenth century coalesced "authorship" and "control" in an intimate relationship (469). This relationship is supported by the vocabulary itself, in "author" as "authority," a word connoting power (470).

Jaszi's point is that literary constructions of authorship muddy application and understanding of authorship in the law. An example of this exists in Michel Foucault's treatment of authorship in his essay "What Is an Author?" Foucault's answer to the titular question substantiates Jaszi's argument when Foucault asks his readers to consider the "author" as a function of discourse, noting that authorship creates propriety: property. Given that Foucault was a Frenchman whose legal base was moral rights and whose background did not include legal training, it is of no surprise that the U.S. law does not operate to uphold this characterization of authorship as creative of property, even though, from a philosophical standpoint, it can, at times, operate as if it does. These dual conceptions of authorship can create confusion, where philosophers and literary critics such as Foucault make assertions from literary perspectives that lead readers to construe a characterization of authorship as a quality imbued in a lauded, powerful, societally supported representative of the status quo, or literary canon, rather than its legal meaning, which confers authorship to creators regardless of their literary or political status.

The imprint of philosophical literary criticism has been influencing interpretation and application of the law, as Jaszi asserts, since the eighteenth century. The way we conceive of authorship influences the way we assign power to creators, and it affects our views of attribution. And literary-philosophical thinking is at its most influential on college campuses, where more professors and their students are likely to read and be affected by this direction of ideas and thus our conception of what authorship means. In fact, Foucault supports the notion that our conceptions of authorship are constructed, when he notes that authorship "is not formed spontaneously through the simple attribution of a discourse to an individual" but results from a complex operation whose purpose is to construct the rational entity we call an author.

Undoubtedly, this construction is assigned a "realistic" dimension as we speak of an individual's "profundity" or "creative" power, his intentions or the original inspiration manifested in writing. (Foucault 127)

And the way we view authorship leads to differences in the way we characterize the work of students, both societally and legally. As a result, members of academic institutions often employ the Romantic concept of authorship, even if unknowingly, when treating student work, so students' legal rights of authorship can go unnoted, because as students, their claim to authorship on the basis of Romantic construction is rarely supported.

The differences between characterizations of authorship in literary-philosophical and legal terms are significant. Literary authorship creates power through author credibility—or historically, through support of an author by powerful patrons—so the authority that comes from authorship, in literary-philosophical terms, resides in authors themselves. Under European law, which continues to reflect Romantic construction of authorship, moral rights are derived from authorship with the idea that the work is attached to the author's personality and expression of his or her innermost being (Jaszi, "Toward a Theory" 497).

Partly in contrast, although current U.S. law provides copyright control to authors and thus gives them the power that comes with it, it also creates authority, control, and power over creative products for those who hold the copyright, whether they are actual authors or not. Under the law, credibility and its validation can reside in holders rather than creators, which is why Slattery's comments regarding the loss of authority in work products of technical communicators as individuals contributing efforts to a range of collaborative teams cannot be assuaged with legal responses. The need for a constructed sense of transcendent authority in authorship declines when the copyright holder has power to validate the creative product. So authorship in literature and authorship in law are treated as two different categories of power, the first, constructed, and the second, assigned.

Academicians who consider authorship through this literary-philosophical lens may be hesitant to conceive of student creators as holders of the powers that reside in authorship. An inability to characterize students as authors can lead to misuse or even abuse of their work, ethically, when applying societal constructions of authorship, and legally, when applying the copyright law. So it is doubly important to examine how we treat student plagiarism and students' copyrights within the academic setting. Several aspects of student academic work arise within the interplay among Romantic characterizations of authorship, plagiarism, and copyright. This section of the chapter treats all three separately but illustrates how each aspect affects the others and how they influence the ways we treat student work. The following material takes into consideration the barriers to viewing students as authors, whose characterization would otherwise attribute authority to their creative work in the same way as it does with validated authors.

Academic systems continue to operate in a way that substantiates power in academic authorship through a system of field-related or communal support that leads to credibility (which comes from accepted authorship) residing within authors themselves. Even among authors with power and authority attached to their work for their own fields, levels of attributed authority vary on the basis of authors' fame, acceptance, or other power traits within their given fields. Outside their own fields, authors' power wanes, and they gather power by whatever means they find available. Some of these means can include attaching themselves to well-respected publishers, being cited by other better accepted authorities, being acknowledged in supportive critiques, or creating extensive support for their work within the communicative documents they create. The last method, gaining power by using extensive source support for their work through citation and other forms of attribution, draws on the authority and power of other authors and, in this way, draws on the power that is attached to others' authority. Attribution in academic settings creates credibility for authors who have little or none, or who are unknown. For new authors such as students, or for those who have not yet been accepted in a field or discipline, extensive attribution can be their only sure source of credibility. In a sense, this operation plays off Foucault's characterization of authorship as property and creates a situation where a validated author retains a commodity of authority in authorship.

Within the Romantic concept, where new authors do not purchase a commoditized credibility, they borrow it by building off the credibility of others. Students, in particular, need the commodity of "purchased" authority because they rarely have authority in their own authorship. The lack of power attributed to students' authorship can cause educators to unwittingly characterize students' works as "property" of the classroom or of the educational institution, and in some cases, educators may even treat students' work as if it were their own.

In addition, instructors who work closely with students as editors and advisors while students create new work may develop a valid sense of authorship in that work when they provide extensive influence through instruction and editing. In the case where instructors overreach, even as a result of impulses to teach well and thoroughly, they may unintentionally create a joint work in which they share authorship with students who do not, on their own, make the effort to develop documents in their own voice, or who refuse to use their own judgments to shape the work. In this case, the Romantic sense of authorship is defeated, particularly in the mind of the instructor who contributed at length to the work's creation.

Certainly, instructors should allow students the room to create their own work, without the interference of overreaching help, even if it means the quality of student-authored work could be poor. But students can only "author" a work to the extent that they take responsibility for its representative qualities of themselves as individuals. For instance, when students create work in which they use others' materials and fail to cite them, they not only commit plagiaristic acts (discussed later in this chapter) but also fail to create authorship. Students are accountable for their own creations and may claim authorship in them only by accepting responsibility through expending their own efforts to develop original work. Students may claim authorship as a commodity only if they create it and are themselves represented by it.

To contemplate commoditization of authorship requires consideration of different kinds of commodities, depending on whether one applies literary-philosophical or legal constructions. Characterizations of the commodity of authorship are distinctly different when perceived from one versus the other construction. A literary-philosophical construction of authorship leads to assessment of the author's inherent power, attaching authority to authorship through the creator's credibility. In this vein of thinking, authors can benefit through their power to influence, to provide desirable advice or opinions to nonauthors, or to teach others how to develop their own paths to authorship and the authority that comes with it, among other possibilities. The authorship commodity is based in part on the author's idea, as well as the expression of the idea, and often the idea and the expression are so melded together that separating them would destroy the essence of the creative work. Under a literary-philosophical treatment of authorship, it is authors' ideas and the authority and credibility in authors themselves that embody the "commodity."

In contrast, under U.S. copyright law, authors have legal control not over ideas but over the expression of those ideas. And the expression of ideas provides authors with control granted through copyright. So it is the copyright rather than the expression itself that is the commodity. The commodity need not be valuable, need not provide the author or its holder with credibility, and need not be supported by others' attributions of worth. These differences in literary-philosophical and legal treatment are significant. And the differences are, in part, why treatment of student work can be inconsistent. Where credibility, authority, and the power of an idea itself reside within an author, it may be difficult for educators to acknowledge that students can be authors, so their work may be treated as insignificant and might be distributed without permission and without ethical consideration for the work as it represents the student.

The dichotomy in literary-philosophical and legal assessment and treatment of authorship and authority is also significant in terms of what distribution can mean for intellectual products and the assignment of authority and power to the work that is distributed. Under both evaluations of authorship and authority, distribution of the "commodity" can benefit the author. But those benefits differ. For authors whose authority comes from credibility, distribution can enlarge and enhance their power (or diminish it by exposing the work to potential criticism). But they can also gain monetarily by selling their expressions for direct monetary benefit. The price of purchase would be relative to the credibility and authority they have in the work produced. Authors control the work when they hold it back, and thus they control access to information, but even when they authorize distribution, under the literary-philosophical assessment of value, authority remains within authors themselves, because they embody the credibility that generates power in the work that is distributed.

Under a literary-philosophical construct, power resides in the credibility of the author, whereas under copyright, power accompanies control of the work. Within copyright, when an author licenses the work to another, the author releases *control* over the work, transferring it to the copyright holder, who decides whether to distribute it and to whom to distribute it. The creator retains some benefit, usually monetary, from licensing the work, but the authority over the work no longer resides within the creator. Of course, actual treatment of intellectual work draws the literary-philosophical and legal treatments of authorship and authority together. And many creators enter legal relationships to license their work to distributors to pursue the benefit of literary-philosophical authority that comes with being published by a company or other organization with credibility, becoming known to the public, and developing credibility and internal authority inherent to authorship itself.

When educators distribute students' works, in violation of the copyright law, circumstances are usually not such that the distribution provides a benefit to students of the sort described above or empowers them as a result of their authorship. To the contrary, using students' work without permission either signifies students' lack of power or, in the act itself, diminishes it.

Authorship under Copyright

Under copyright law that treats subjects of literary expression, ideas are not protected against use by other than the author; instead, only the author's expression of ideas can be protected. Moreover, under the law, with the legal fiction of work for hire, the fictional author may not have even developed the idea. So even though the idea is attributed to the actual author, he or she under the legal fiction may not maintain the power to control the expression. This differing characterization of authorship under the law is significant in that the law essentially disregards the transcendental power attributed through Romantic conceptualization of authorship; it also disregards the process of providing benefit to the creator. Instead, it favors utility in assigning power to those who control and distribute the work. Even so, in the literary sense, authors can retain their authority, and thus power of authorship, through reputation. So when publishers retain copyrights and take control of the work for distribution, the author's credibility and internal power remains intact, even though the copyright—and its control of the expression itself—transfers to the hands of publishers. The statute states,

> In no case does copyright protection for an original work of authorship extend to any idea, procedure, process, system, method of operation, concept, principle, or discovery, regardless of the form in which it is described, explained, illustrated, or embodied in such work. (1976 Copyright Act, §102[b])

U.S copyright law provides means for protecting expressions but not the ideas behind them. Copyright allows its holders to decide who can use, copy, and disseminate the expressions that an author has created. But it provides no means to control the idea. Instead, extralegal moral and ethical codes are used to provide a base for protection of authors' efforts in developing original thought. And although patent has not in the past protected ideas (See *Diamond v. Diehr, Gottschalk v. Benson, Funk Bros. Seed Co. v. Kalo Inoculant Co.*, and *Rubber-Tip Pencil Co. v. Howard* in E. Samuels), there is a developing trend in that direction today (*Apple Computer, Inc. v. Franklin Computer Corp.* and *Nat'l. Med. Care, Inc. v. Espiritu* in Bathaee).

(Although a subject of interesting discussion, its treatment at length is not within the purpose of this work.)

Students are best prepared to deal with all the complexities of authorship and use of materials when they understand the differences between copyright and plagiarism and learn how their own work is affected by them.

Plagiarism

As noted above, in the literary-philosophical consideration of authorship, it is the author's ideas that are prized, sometimes even more than the expression of those ideas. So protecting authorship in literary structures requires a system of sanctions for plagiarism, because sanctions against plagiarism protect ideas as much as they do authors' expressions. Although the expression of ideas embodies the ideas themselves and the expression can be so merged that the expression is the idea and the idea is the expression, the value placed in literary-philosophical assessment of authorship resides in the authority of the ideas. So plagiarism is used as an appropriate structure for protecting authors' authority as it resides in their ideas. For example, to meet the requirements of one of the assignments for my intellectual property class, one of my students created a machinima, a digital role-playing mechanism of machine animation used in virtual worlds such as World of Warcraft. Her machinima embodied commentary regarding intellectual property law and machinima in a way that was self-parodic, both in its form as a commentary on copyright and machinima, as well as its existence as a machinima in which it spoke to issues of copyright. Both the idea and the expression was the machinima itself. My student's work, as her original idea, expressed her authorship, and the work and its successful content and existence in visually accessible digital form expressed her authority.

But not all students achieve the quality of authorship in the work they submit in classes. Educators claim to be facing a crisis of student plagiarism today, asserting that abuses of authors' works is reaching new highs, citing studies that show that "more than 70 percent of college students admit to some cheating, and more than half of the 2100 students surveyed admitted to 'serious cheating on written assignments,'" and other surveys that showed that that 50 percent of the students surveyed admitted to plagiarizing from the Internet while others reported using paper mills as a source for class work (Dickerson 21). One researcher cites studies showing that of more than two thousand students from twenty-one colleges polled, 10 percent admitted to "borrowing" materials and 5 percent reported that they had used parts of works or whole papers and passed them off as their own (Gerdy 431).

Plagiarism, unlike copyright, provides an ethical or moral system for protecting authors' work. "The parameters of the modern definition of plagiarism emerged during the late eighteenth century out of the Romantic emphasis on individualism and the conviction that writers are obligated to make unique contributions to any material" (Stearns 517). Where ideas are not protected in copyright, they are under rules prohibiting plagiarism. At times, either copyright law or plagiarism prohibitions can apply to work that is so merged with expression that both systems apply, particularly where the ideas, not protected under copyright, are so merged with the expression, protected under copyright. In this case, both systems apply. Plagiarism occurs when a person takes the ideas or expressions of another and passes them off as his or her own.

Copyright's protections are very different, where they allow authors to prevent others from copying, distributing, or creating derivative works from their copyrighted originals. But copyright also provides mechanisms that allow authors to inhibit others' use of their work in visual materials such as those that may be produced by technical communication or digital media students. In addition to providing a means to prohibit another from mutilating or distorting an original work in a way that would harm a creator's reputation, this right of attribution and integrity provides a means to prohibit another from attributing authorship to an original creator's work if that work's character was modified. This aspect of copyright, which provides control of a work in terms of its attribution (§106A), allows authors to protect their reputations to help ensure that they would not be misrepresented; in this way, this inhibition in copyright reflects forms of limitation similar to those that sanctions against plagiarism provide. Nevertheless, it extends to the expression only and not the idea behind it. And this form of protection, like all other copyright protections, is still subject to parody and free speech limitations, where others may create new works based on the original as a basis for critical comment.

Copyright infringements can occur even when the user makes clear that the infringed work was not his or her own authored work, where plagiarism can occur only when the violator makes it appear that he or she is the author. Again, plagiarism addresses the commodity of authorship in credibility, where copyright treats the commodity of control over the intellectual product. Copyright is an infringement based on use, where plagiarism is a violation of representation. In essence, plagiarism violates the person, where copyright infringes the object. Plagiarists claim to be who or what they are not, where infringers of copyright claim to have the right to use an expression in a way that they do not. One author's description of plagiarism (although applied in a different context) is helpful for understanding the distinction:

> [P]lagiarism is a failure of the creative process, not a flaw in its result. Although imitation is an inevitable component of creation, plagiarists pass beyond the boundaries of acceptable imitation by copying from the work of others without improving upon the copied material or fully assimilating it into their own work; by failing to attribute the copied material to its actual author; and by intending to deceive others about its origin. Society's disapproval is directed toward the plagiarist and the process of plagiarism, not toward the result. (Stearns 520)

The distinctions between plagiarism and copyright infringement are significant, particularly when students are learning to use sources as a means to understand new concepts and to support their own work when they respond to what they have learned. Accessing and interacting with sources in the process of learning is usually not problematic, since much of students' academic work is supported by the law that might otherwise inhibit them. But using the material to create intellectual products can be problematic when students fail to acknowledge which parts of the products are their own and which were created by another author.

Simply put, student creators can avoid plagiarism by adding citations to all others' work that is used within their own. And copyright users can avoid violation by using work in ways that the Constitution and fair use allow. (See chapter 2, where copyright issues are discussed at length.) Of course, in neither case is it always clear when work must be cited or when use is or is not allowed. In each distinct instance, the context surrounding uses of others' work determines whether use is supportable under ethical or legal structures.

Students may create works that rely on remix, and they may develop parodies, multimedia work, and even music that is synthesized with other work. Much of what they create can fall within fair use protections. But not all educational work, regardless of format, digital or hard-copy, can be created without attribution to sources, especially when attributions allow students to avoid plagiarism. Particularly when their work is developed in the process of learning, students still can and should attribute sources, even if those sources are attributed through the style of the work itself. Part of their learning effort is to better understand and become comfortable with choices they make when treating others' works. When in doubt students should provide citations for the work they use; even in the development of a remix, a creator can include citations to portions of others' work, either within the remix by noting the original or at the end of the work in a list of sources used.

Students can provide these citations within hard copy or digital documents, and in multimedia pieces, they could make creative use of technology by including rollovers or other digital mechanisms that show the source of their materials, or employing some other technique that enhances the work rather than hampering it. When a work is so transformed that an author can see only influence in a work rather than a piece of the original work itself, the student could most likely comfortably avoid citation. But students and their professors both should beware when making the decision not to cite sources.

Professors should also be careful not to misuse students' works or each others', particularly because their actions can be seen as examples for student behavior. And students have an ethical duty not to violate the copyright of other students' work or to plagiarize each other. Plagiarism is based not in the law but in ethical duty. An author not only is a holder of legal rights but also retains the inherent connection to the created work as the embodiment of the author him- or herself. Both professors and students have a societal duty to attribute authorship to the creator who developed the original inventive product.

Students, and even professors, may think that an author's permission to use the copyright of a work can also function as permission to use the work without attribution. So where a student works collaboratively with others on a document for one class and then, with permission of the collaborative team, reuses the material for another class, claiming authorship in the work, he or she may assume that the act is not one of plagiarism. In fact, to avoid plagiarism, the student must attribute authorship to each member of the collaborative team who produced the original document.

It is possible for an author to grant a copyright license in a work that would provide another with the legal right to use, copy, disseminate, and create a derivative work from the original work; but the original creator cannot provide a right for another author to claim the work as his or her own origination. The nature of authorship is such that attribution is always required to avoid plagiarism, whether a copyright license is provided or not. Both students and their professors should be fully aware of the potential ramifications of choices they make in using others' work.

There are many different reasons why students plagiarize, and some explanations are more forgivable than others. Among those that indict the educational systems as much as the students are situations in which students are unaware of what plagiarism is or in which they have not understood well how to distinguish times when there is a need to cite sources or when citation is unnecessary in cases such as use of material considered common knowledge. Some students may not understand that even paraphrased material has to be attributed to its author.

Other instances of plagiarism can arise when students take notes poorly and are careless about adding cite notations in early stages of information gathering or careless about adding quotation marks around that which is directly quoted. One author points out how simple it would be to eliminate a good portion of plagiarized work, where, "[i]n the academic world, plagiarism arises most often as unattributed use of material that, were it properly credited, would not be considered plagiaristic at all" (Stearns).

Other authors who have considered plagiarism list additional reasons why students plagiarize, including the excessive workload or the mindless nature of academic work they are asked to undertake, the influence of cultural backgrounds that induce them to plagiarize, the existence of opportunity, and the effect of influence by prominent individuals who cheat (Thomas 426–27). In addition, some note that students may "feel that assembling sources, citations, and quotes is the primary goal of writing a paper and that their original ideas are secondary" (Whitaker [1993] in DeVoss and Rosati 195).

Some note that students plagiarize knowingly, thinking they can get away with it or because the political climate of dishonesty makes students' plagiarism seem trivial (Gerdy 432) or because students feel that they are unlikely to be caught because their professors will not bother to deal with it (434). And in the case of students who buy papers from services that provide them with the work of others,

> [t]oo many students—and sometimes their parents—are more concerned about getting a certain grade or obtaining a degree than achieving competency and learning to learn. They view a "college education" as a mere commodity, as a ticket that has to be punched on their way to a career in corporate America. (Dickerson 24)

More complex reasons why students might plagiarize relate to differences in expectations for citation from one situation to another. Law review journals require extensive documentation, even to the extent that their editors are uncomfortable when an author makes a statement on his or her own authority (Thomas 424). In contrast, in news media, "repurposing" of traditional news stories into nontraditional formats is considered appropriate "when practiced correctly" (Muller 84).

The differing contexts for when to use and cite sources can be confusing, particularly to inexperienced authors. Attributions in citations and other forms of quoting and acknowledging sources are important for those who are not powerful enough to write without them. But well-known authors are often able to make statements without support because their reputations as knowledgeable in their disciplines allow them to make statements as experts in themselves. Students who try to imitate the authors whose works they study may be surprised and confused to find that they need more research support and citations than their models do. Students would be helped by realizing that not only do they cite sources to avoid plagiarism but also, and more important, they use citations to support the arguments and claims they make. Their need to provide citation and the support of others' materials changes as they become more academically sophisticated.

Graduate students in particular may experience changes in how they treat citation and support for work. They may find that early in their academic careers, before they are able to distinguish between what is common knowledge in their field and what is not, they should cite nearly every piece of information they use. But as they become more experienced, they may find themselves more capable of recognizing unattributed repeated concepts in the majority of their sources, which indicates that the material can be considered common knowledge, and may find that they will gradually be able to cite fewer passages in the material they research.

Other, not so forgivable reasons that students plagiarize include the pressures of deadlines that students cannot meet either because they have a large amount of work in many classes or because they have procrastinated. Some students also feel inadequate to the tasks they have to meet in class and plagiarize to "get it right," whereas others are just lazy. "[W]hile experts agree that new technology has made plagiarizing easier for students, they disagree whether the 'ease' of cyberplagiarsm has led to an increase in its occurrence" (Gerdy 432). Some plagiarism is intentional and some not, and it is not clear whether a user's intent is required for a misuse of another work to be considered plagiarism (Stearns 532–34). Some argue, however, that it should require intent (Green 182). Regardless, harshness of the sanctions employed as punishment for plagiarism are relative to whether evidence shows that a user had knowledge of or intent to plagiarize, and sometimes a question arises regarding whether an accused plagiarist was so negligent in noting source attribution that the negligence itself would be punishable as plagiarism. Recently, historians Doris Kearns Goodwin and Stephen Ambrose have defended themselves against accusations of plagiarism.

In Stephen Ambrose's case, a 2002 *Weekly Standard* article pointed to several passages in Ambrose's *The Wild Blue Yonder: The Men and Boys Who Flew the B-24s over Germany* that mirrored, almost verbatim, passages from Thomas Childers's *Wings of Morning: The Story of the Last American Bomber Shot Down over Germany in World War II* (Nelson 383). Ambrose apologized but admitted to sloppy work rather than plagiarism. He explained that his grown children had helped him with his research because he had created eight books in five years and he confused some of the notes, failing to add quotation marks around the quoted material (Nelson 384). After the apology, other reporters uncovered a number of other instances of unquoted copied work in several of Ambrose's books. Over time and after close scrutiny of a number of Ambrose's books, reporters revealed instances dating back to the 1960s, before Ambrose was well known and before his initial excuse would hold up (Nelson 385).

The story of Doris Kearns Goodwin is similar to Ambrose's. Her book, *The Fitzgeralds and the Kennedys: An American Saga*, contained a number of mirrored passages from Hank Searls's *The Lost Prince: Young Joe, the Forgotten Kennedy*, Rose Kennedy's autobiography, *Times to Remember*, and Lynne McTaggert's *Kathleen Kennedy: Her Life and Times*. Goodwin apologized but downplayed the extent of use of others' work. Having made most extensive use of McTaggert's work without footnoting or crediting her, Goodwin finally negotiated a settlement in response to McTaggert's threats of a lawsuit (Nelson 385–86).

When an unattributed idea is so widespread that it becomes assimilated into society, it is difficult to know what is and is not original and citable material, particularly when it comes to mind in a new author who is not aware of the source. All authors create work based on multiple societal influences and experiences, many of which every author shares, so it is nearly impossible to create completely new thoughts and sometimes even new expressions. It is certainly not inconceivable that an author would have a "new" idea that already existed. As one author notes, there is a fuzzy line between plagiarism and "mere influence" (Green 178), where "it is not always easy to distinguish between writing that is copied with the intent of being passed off as the plagiarist's own and writing that is merely subject to the inadvertent 'influence' of earlier work" (Green 171). David Thomas explains well how society's influence affects authorship:

> People do not shape their words and ideas in a vacuum. Authors of professional and scholarly research and writing are constantly seeking out and reflecting on the words, ideas, and data from other sources and other authors in an effort to form their own words and ideas. In ordinary research and writing activities, writers cite to sources for elements of thoughts and expressions they know they could not

have created on their own, and also for support or confirmation of their own thoughts and expressions. It is also common for writers to subconsciously repeat catchy or common phrases that came to their attention from other sources. They almost never think of their own thoughts and expressions as having been borrowed or copied, even though they are obviously composites of their reading, conversations, observation, and experience. If one considers these common practices in light of the short and simple definitions of plagiarism . . . , then almost everyone is guilty of plagiarism all the time. (Thomas 422)

In truth, we all express ourselves by building on ideas and expressions of others, because the necessities of communication rely on common understanding. In an extreme but illustrative incidence of accused plagiarism against Helen Keller in "Touching Words: Helen Keller, Plagiarism, Authorship," Jim Swan describes how Helen Keller came to be accused of plagiarism after publishing her story "The Frost King." Swan explains how, deaf and dumb, Keller was able to exchange ideas, essentially speak, by memorizing especially communicative phrases and sentences from works that were read to her and then reuse the phrases and sentences to describe her thoughts and state of mind to interact with others. That these phrases and sentences were verbatim quotes from other works was the source of her problems with plagiarism. Although Keller's case was extreme, and she would not have been able to communicate at all without using this unique means of expression, her experience reflects that of all authors who build from prior communications and expressions, and the expressions used communicate much deeper messages to viewers, listeners, and readers than would be possible without them. Drawing new comments from prior comments is a part of cultural interchange that allows an extension of communication on multiple levels.

In a classic example, Jimi Hendrix not only provided an artistic reflection of the country's disarray but also created new commentary and political statement in protest of the Vietnam war and the lack of civil rights through his transformative performance of the "Star Spangled Banner" at Woodstock in 1969. Although the music itself was not his own, his rendition changed it drastically and supported his statement of protest in a deeply meaningful way. Another, lighter example points to the popular television program *Gilmore Girls*, which is well known for its use of catchphrases and prior-used expressions as a base for humor, commentary, and sometimes political speech. These are not instances of plagiarism but works of artists interacting with societal ideas as a means of expressing something new.

So what is plagiarism in light of the ways we interact with information at the turn of the new century? Much more complex issues lead to potential plagiarism, including those that mirror a shift in how we treat information. Stuart Green points to ways in which plagiarism is recharacterized today to complicate ways we conceive of plagiarism:

> Some scholars have argued that the rule against plagiarism itself is obsolete. One point emphasized by scholars in the postmodernist tradition is that the line between plagiarism and acceptable forms of copying is not always easy to discern. Such theorists have tended to recast conduct that might have otherwise been stigmatized as plagiarism with morally neutral, even morally favorable, terms such as "voice merging," "echoing," "intertextualizing," "synthesizing," "textual appropriation," "resonance," and "patchwriting." Some have even gone so far as to suggest that the idea of the "author" or "artist" as lone "genius" is most appropriately viewed as an artifact of capitalist, colonialist, even racist and sexist ideology. (Green 179)

Part of the shift in views of authorship today may reflect how we value information and its source. Where in the eighteenth century, Romantic authorship was the basis for esteem, credibility, and power, "the notion of 'authorship' and 'originality' emerged as significant cultural values" (Green 176). But today, in a time when even the value of information has declined because it can become stale in a matter of weeks or days, its authorship becomes that much less important, particularly to students whose first choice of tool for research activities, news gathering, long-distance person-to-person interaction, and often entertainment, is the Internet, where authorship is underplayed. Beyond Internet-based research tools provided by libraries, the Internet provides a broad spectrum of means to gather and interact with information in the forms of text, images, videos, music, and software, among others.

The more functional blogs that are prevalent today provide means for viewers to access the latest commentary on new information and its values and for users to interact by providing new information or agreeing with, contradicting, or expanding on what others have written. For the casual reader-viewer, author attribution in blogs is unimportant and does not drive their return to a blogspot. For a blogger who is highly invested in the topic or the site, the esteem that comes with authorship can be developed over time, but the basis for the interactions are in the "come one, come all" inclusive approach to a means for providing information to a public that is not likely to be attentive or even aware of a blog's authorship. For example, all the content of Wikipedia, an online encyclopedia project, is made of contributions by thousands of unnamed authors that, through a process of informal argument and review available to all comers regardless of background or education, provide surprisingly accurate information. It describes itself: "Wikipedia is a multilingual, web-based, free content encyclopedia project. Wikipedia is written collaboratively by volunteers; the vast majority of its articles can be edited by anyone with access to the Internet." Wikipedia makes no claims about the authority in its authorship, and its millions of users seem not to mind.

Another response to authorship in a nontraditional vein is hip-hop music and the sampling practices that it involves. Sampling in hip-hop music does prize authorship in the artist who claims the title but includes multiple sources of work within it, acting as references to ideas, concepts, and aural means to conjure up responses in listeners either to the counterplay of a sample to the source or in referencing a theme noted in the sampled work. These portions of sampled works are not attributed, in part because they act in the same ways for hip-hop listeners as literary allusions act for readers of literature. One author notes that when hip-hop artists mix sample pieces with their work and violate the structure of Romantic authorship by leaving out source attributions, they are, in some part, claiming a part of the culture that may or may not have be open to them before. These are prized as acts of renegade justice, to some extent (Hess).

The YouTube phenomenon is yet another example of a technology that has grown popular, in part, because it depends on voluntary postings by individuals who have interesting or entertaining ideas and bypass traditional publishing mechanisms to make them available to the public. YouTube has experienced its share of legal problems with those who have posted video clips from copyrighted sources without permission from holders, another indication of a new attitude toward the efficacy of power in authorship. But it has also provided a means to share political commentary and the ability to use copyrighted material as the base for that commentary. For example, average citizen "LiberalViewer" created a montage of video clips from Fox news broadcasts to show that when it aired a portion of *The Daily Show*'s commentary on George Bush, it edited out all political critical content, and another average citizen, "hayabusa," provided YouTube video showing college Republicans' support for George Bush in Portland, Oregon.

The popularity of sites like these, as well as others that support independent films and independent bands, are indicative of a general push to bypass commercial means of popularizing products through the manufacture of credibility in authorship. Instead, these new mechanisms allow unknown creators with no inherent power or credibility to bypass the traditional systems and develop audiences on the basis of the product itself. Today, independent status adds cachet rather than destroying it.

In the rare case when credibility through popular acceptance does attach to the author who contributed a YouTube piece or who produced a popular blog, the Romantic concept of authorship is reified. And students may have a special interest in this form of authorship because they are often producers of the work that becomes popular. But for the most part, these examples and others like them indicate a shift away from a Romantic treatment of authorship to one in which authorship is less important than the information or products that it produces. Students of technical communication and digital media, as well as those who work in other fields with a particular interest in visual rhetoric and production, may have a special interest in user-generated visual content and may find venues such as YouTube a significant source of information for research, entertainment, and inspiration. And students, who are often primary audiences of these venues, are affected by the attitudinal change represented.

It is not surprising that students might value (or devalue) authorship as a result of cultural shifts due to interaction with digital materials in making and using creative work. Digitization creates a less personal attachment of authorship to products when they are remixed, shaped, and influenced by multiple parties. As such, the digital culture that supports this kind of interaction with products can shape students' views of authorship. Moreover, in more subtle ways, likely even those of which students are unaware, their responses to and interaction with hyperculture may lead them to operate with sources in a way that in itself is a reconsideration of authority in authorship and ultimately influences how society assesses the value of authorship. In postacademic settings, former students may eventually affect the law itself by changing it to adapt to views of authorship influenced by digital culture. Nevertheless, students must learn the pragmatic skills necessary to avoid plagiarism and support their creative work with sources while proffering their own new contributions to knowledge. And educators are in an optimal position to help them do this, particularly since claims of a significant amount of deliberate plagiarism today are growing (Green 187).

Some authors who have considered the problematic nature of plagiarism have suggested means to inhibit it on college campuses. And when students encounter legal problems with copyright they may still find that traditional means of attaching value to authorship affect the outcome of conflicts. "That Romantic 'authorship' is alive and well in late twentieth-century American legal culture has consequences for the law's engagement with (or failure to engage) the realities of contemporary polyvocal writing practice—which increasingly is collective, corporate, and collaborative" (Jaszi, "On the Author Effect" 38). So students must beware the consequences of their being educated within a time in which considerations of authorship are influenced by both the old and new centuries.

Legal educators and communication instructors suggest many ways to detect student plagiarism. Some say that instructors should know their students' work well so that they will easily become aware of changes in syntax, style, and linguistic choices to cue work not produced by the potential student plagiarist (Gerdy 434). Others suggest that educators should be aware of the work within their own disciplines so that they can easily recognize work that is reproduced from their own banks of articles and books (Thomas 428), and one author suggests that professors search databases for key words in students' work but asserts that this method would require that professors assume that every student has plagiarized (Dickerson 60–61). Students are sometimes also aware that others may attempt to plagiarize their own work and can have a particular interest in locating those who would do so.

Among other means for detecting plagiarism are the following potential indicators: an instructor senses something familiar about a paper, the paper style changes, formatting or font changes exist in the paper, citation formats are inconsistent, the work lacks recent references or includes unusual references, or the student is unable to discuss the content of the work (Gerdy 434–35). Because plagiarism is difficult to detect, many authors suggest using commercial plagiarism detection databases such as CopyCatchGold, CopyFind, WordCheck, and Turnitin.com. The following section discusses why these databases may not well serve the interests of educators who use them and how their use could be both unethical and infringing of students' work.

Turnitin.com and Other Infringing Databases

Some educators who look for means to deter plagiarism among students have turned to plagiarism detection services such as CopyCatch, Eve2, and Turnitin.com. These services vary in their operation, so they also vary in their legality and ethicality. Most plagiarism detection services provide a means for professors to test their students' text submissions through a program that checks the text against text on the Internet, but Turnitin.com is more controversial because it retains copies of students' work in its database and compares database materials against one another. It is by far the most widely used of these plagiarism detection services and "receives over 100,000 student papers per day" (Turnitin.com). Its own Web site notes that its structure is used by "thousands of Institutions [*sic*] in over eighty countries" and that it searches "billions of pages from both current and archived instances of the internet, millions of student papers previously submitted to Turnitin.com, and commercial databases of journal articles and periodicals."

It is also the most controversial and potentially the most abusive of students' rights. At this writing, Turnitin.com's site operation depends on submission of students' works stored on its database to provide a source for comparison of students' work worldwide. The company's software compares student documents with others in the database, which instructors and administrators use as a tool to uncover plagiarized text. Plagiarism detection databases that are structured as this one can violate students' copyrights and can result in ethical harm as well.

To examine reasons to refrain from using databases such as this, it is helpful to revisit discussion of copyright, explained in the first chapter. Under controlling U.S. copyright law, authors—even student authors of intellectual products—retain copyrights in their works without the need for registration. U.S. copyright law does not require that intellectual products be of good quality to be copyrightable, so the quality of authorship (i.e., its credibility and authority or lack thereof in the authors themselves) is of no consequence for initial grant of copyright. That the quality of students' work might not be on par with their instructors' or professors', or professional authors', is not a determining factor in their grant of copyright protection for the work. Student copyright holders, like others, have the right to copy and distribute their work and to make derivative works from them, as well as to *prevent others from copying, distributing, or making derivative works from their intellectual products*, among other rights.

Students, when acting as students, by definition, are not employees of their educational institutions. But they sometimes undertake extracurricular work activities for their institutions and in this capacity may be characterized as employees. Where the intellectual products they create in their capacity as students cannot be considered works for hire, which would provide their institutions with corporate authorship and copyright control, products they create within the scope of their duties as employees can.

Where students may have an implied contract to allow their instructors to read and respond to their work, grade it, check it for plagiarism, and even share it with other students within the class for purposes of teaching and learning, this implied contract does not extend to third parties, particularly when those parties' interest is in commercial benefit from students' work.

Students must knowingly provide consent to license terms and must have bargaining power to negotiate for those terms in order for licenses to be valid. And in fact, professors may well have a fiduciary duty, a special duty of care, to treat their students' work carefully because students' bargaining power may be limited in light of their professors' capacity as authoritative figures to affect students' futures in significant ways (discussed in detail in the conclusion).

Educators who use plagiarism detection services and do not consider student rights in their intellectual products could find themselves violating student copyrights, as well as their ethical (and fiduciary) duties to students, and might eventually find themselves embroiled in legal conflict when students choose to take action. Plagiarism detection services claim that their use of students' work to support their companies' actions is not harmful, and one such service, Turnitin.com, reported to have the largest number of subscribers and students' intellectual products in its database files, has provided a paper containing its claimed legal justifications for using student work. Because Turnitin.com's justifications are representative of those that a broad range of detection services could use and because discussion of these claims illustrates how copyright in students' work can be understood, the following section lists Turnitin.com's claims regarding copyright, accompanied by responses and discussion of each claim. These statements represent a response to Turnitin.com's justifications that were accessible at this writing.

Turnitin.com states,

> Note that copyright issues are only raised with respect to any aspect of the Turnitin.com system if the work submitted qualifies for copyright protection. See 17 U.S.C. §§ 102 and 106 (copyright provides the holder with the right to exclude others from reproducing, preparing derivative works from, distributing copies of, performing or displaying an original work of authorship). A student's contribution to a test paper on which selections have been made among answers to multiple choice questions clearly falls well short of the "original authorship" necessary to give the student a copyright in the completed test paper. (Turnitin.com section 4)

Turnitin.com's implication that students' work would not qualify for copyright protection is misleading, since the student work submitted for comparison to detect plagiarism is not that which Turnitin.com describes above. Neither students nor their instructors submit multiple-choice tests to Turnitin.com to detect plagiarism, because there would be no potential for plagiarism in choosing a number or letter from a series of choices. But Turnitin.com continues,

> Even short essays may, if primarily consisting of factual recitations, be free of any copyright interest. 17 U.S.C. § 102(b). Therefore, this discussion pertains primarily to more extensive compositions in which a putative copyright interest may be present in some or all of the work. (Turnitin.com 4)

Again, this statement is misleading. Although it is true that facts themselves are not copyrightable, using facts in a work, regardless of length, does not necessarily disqualify it from copyright protection. A database of facts in the form of a compilation can be protectable on the basis that the copyright exists in the expression of facts.

Turnitin.com asserts,

> If copyright is present in a particular student's work, the submission of the work to a teacher as part of the student's coursework necessarily carries with it the expectation that the teacher will use the work in certain ways, consistent with the goal of evaluating and grading the student's work. Specifically, by submitting the work, the student implicitly agrees that the teacher may comment on, criticize and otherwise evaluate the academic quality of the work, an evaluation that should include consideration of both the work's content and integrity. . . . In some institutions, school policy reduces this "implied license" to use a work for academic evaluation to writing by, for example, specifying that teachers may receive, copy, or distribute student works. Whether written or implied, such evaluation licenses carry with them certain collateral rights, to the extent necessary to the enjoyment of the right granted to perform the evaluation. See legal authorities referenced above [cited and discussed below to allow discussion of each part of Turnitin.com's assertions]. Such collateral rights might include, for example, the right to make a copy of the work to enable others to evaluate it (e.g., a teaching assistant), the right to image the work for computerized grading (e.g., tests written on scannable test forms) or, as is true of dissertations and theses, the right to archive the work in a publicly accessible collection.

There is no explicit legal support for applying the concept of implied license in student work, but the concept is accepted in other areas of interchange, although commercial, and could be used as logical support for the interactions of educators and students that allow learning processes. Neverthe-less, an educational institution's determination of what the implied license would allow is not law and not enforceable as such. Given that there must be a kind of implied license that would allow the educational process to go forward, it is important to assess to whom an implied license would extend and for what purposes. Students enter educational institutions with expectations that they will produce work for classes and that it will be graded by their instructors or teaching assistants, potentially examined by administrators, and used as a basis for evaluation to further their learning. They would even expect that the work could be examined by educators for purposes of detecting plagiarism.

Students would not expect, and an implied license would not extend to the possibility, that students' work would be provided to a commercial entity outside the educational setting, especially when unlicensed copies would allow the commercial entity to profit from students' work without their permission. Moreover, where an implied license extends to educators' justification to make personal use of students' work within the educational process, copyright law allows license holders to prohibit a user, even an instructor, from distributing and making derivative works from their in-tellectual products without permission. So an instructor who receives a student's paper in support of work in class can grade it and might even make a copy of it to do so, but the law would not support the actions of an instructor who provided the work to a publisher, posted it on the Internet (with access outside the classroom) for others to view, or created a new work from the original. But again, professors' fiduciary duties to students should limit their ability to impose undue force on students to treat their work in ways they find unacceptable.

To support its claim that educators retain an implied license to do with students' papers what they want, Turnitin.com refers to

> Foad Consulting Group, supra at 828–831 (copying, distribution and modification of a work to make it usable for the intended purpose necessarily a part of the implied license to use the work); as well as Recording Industries Ass'n of Am. V. Diamond Multimedia Sys., Inc., 180 F.3d 1072, 1079 (9th Cir. 1999) (transfer of a work, such as music, into another media, such as an MP3 file, for personal use of the person making the transfer is a fair use), and Sony Corp. v. Universal City Studios, Inc., 464 U.S. 417, 449–50 (1984) (copying of broadcast productions onto videotape for later viewing using a VCR is a fair use); compare, A&M Records, Inc., et al. v. Napster, Inc., 239 F.3d 1004, 1019 (9th Cir. 2001) (copying of a work for personal use not

fair when coupled to simultaneous distribution of the entire work to the general public)

and states,

> Hence, by itself, teacher submission of a student work to Turnitin.com is within the scope of the evaluation license provided by the student to the teacher on submission of the work for grading. The implied license may not extend to other aspects of the Turnitin.com system, such as archiving; however, such aspects are allowable as "fair uses" of the copyrighted material.

The case law that Turnitin.com references pertains to contractual relationships between commercial entities or treats individuals' personal use for noncommercial purposes, and it also uses for support the Ninth Circuit's decision in *A&M Records v. Napster,* which has now been distinguished by new cases, discussed above. These cases that Turnitin.com cites are inapplicable to students' work in several areas. Unlike the commercial relationships these cases above represent, students do not enter into negotiated contracts to determine how their work will be used in educational institutions. In addition, they do not provide coursework for commercial purposes. And educators' interactions with students' work products is intended not to create marketable, commercial products but to use student products as a basis for teaching and learning. Beyond problems with the case law above, Turnitin.com once again indicates that an implied license that a student may provide to educators extends to Turnitin.com. An implied license, in any case, exists between or among parties to the interaction that creates it and not to third parties. In the case of students who may provide implied licenses to educators, the license is sure not to extend to commercial entities who profit from students' work without their permission to use it.

Turnitin.com's claim in the last sentence, that using students' work to submit it to plagiarism detection services is fair use, is repeated in several instances in Turnitin.com's legal justifications, and each is dealt with in turn, below:

> It is possible, albeit unlikely, that institutional or class policy may negate such an implied license [to use students' work] by explicitly prohibiting all third party use of student works, absent student consent. Even then, a teacher's use of Turnitin.com would likely still be considered fair use, as the purpose of the evaluation is to provide personal assistance to the teacher for his or her educational, non-commercial

use, and the work itself is not released to the public until and unless the author consents to its publication. (Turnitin.com 7)

Fair use is provided to users as a means to advance learning, not to police textual transgressions. The doctrine is in place to support a public domain that allows citizens to access information from which to learn, about which to comment, and about which to report. It provides a means for educators and students to access information in order to learn from it or speak about it. Where an instructor or student copied two works to explain plagiarism by using them in illustrative juxtapositions, the purpose of fair use would most likely be upheld. But when educators use students' work without permission, not as a basis for learning, illustration of ideas or concepts, or other uses noted in the doctrine but instead to create evidence of violative activity, their actions would not fall within the intention of fair use. Where instructors may not use students' work for their own commercial benefit, Turnitin.com, through the instructors' provision of work, surely does. In this way, instructors become procurers of students' work in support of Turnitin.com's potentially illegal activity.

Turnitin.com also claims that its archiving of student work, keeping copies of students' intellectual products on its databases, is fair use because it does so for educational purposes (Turnitin.com 7) and asserts that the use is nonprofit and does not affect marketability of students' work (8). But Turnitin.com is not nonprofit and it retains students' work in its databases for commercial benefit. In fact, Turnitin.com sells its services to educators who use the service to aid in policing activity peripheral to educational efforts; where teaching about plagiarism and discussing issues regarding authorship and intellectual property policy and law would be educational activities, detecting plagiarism is not a learning process but evidence gathering activity. In an interview for the *Chronicle of Higher Education*, law professor Dan Burk responded to Turnitin.com's claim of fair use:

> "That's baloney." As many as three factors undermine the argument, . . . The students' papers are completely copied. They are often creative works, as opposed to compilations of scientific facts. And they are being submitted to a commercial enterprise, not an educational institution. "To run a database, you've got to make a copy, and if the student hasn't authorized that, then that's potentially an infringing copy," says Mr. Burk. (Foster a37)

Turnitin.com also describes its process of using a copy of students' works to create a "fingerprint" that allows its system to compare data for plagiarism detection. It claims that the "fingerprint" of the work is not the work itself, so in using it, there is no copyright violation. But, first, to create the "fingerprint," Turnitin.com has to have used or made a copy of the students' work and if that copy is made or used without the student's permission, it is a copyright violation. Second, the "fingerprint" is created—derived—from the student's work, so Turnitin.com would infringe the students' copyright by making a derivative work without the students' license to do so.

Most arguments that Turnitin.com makes in attempt to justify its use of student work are based on a rhetorical fiction that the company stands in the place of the educator and retains the qualities, purposes, and noncommercial attributes of the instructor teaching students within the educational system. At the March 2009 meeting of CCCC's Intellectual Property Caucus, Katie Povejsil, vice president of marketing for iParadigms claimed that Turnitin.com is not a plagiarism detection service but a teaching tool. But commercial services whose economic health depend on submissions of student work for comparison such as Turnitin.com's are in the business not of educating students but rather providing a commercial service to others. Where educators generally do not profit by copying or using their students' intellectual products, companies like Turnitin.com do. And students, including most who do not plagiarize but whose work is copied and distributed without permission, are affected negatively when their legal rights in copyright are disregarded.

Despite reasoning that would support students' rights in their work, in March 2008, the District Court for the Eastern District of Virginia disregarded students' rights by holding in favor of iParadigms (Turnitin.com's owner and operator) in *A. V. et al., Plaintiffs, v. iParadigms, Limited Liability Company*. In this case, four students from Virginia and Arizona high schools sued Turnitin.com for violating the copyrights in their work produced to satisfy school assignments. The students were required to submit their class assignments to Turnitin.com or receive a grade of zero on their work. The Web-based submission process required students to click an "I agree" button to produce seeming acquiescence to the terms of the clickwrap agreement, which, in addition to allowing Turnitin.com to copy and reproduce their work, provided a limitation-of-liability clause in favor of Turnitin.com.

The students submitted their assignments to Turnitin.com rather than receive a grade of zero but included a written disclaimer on their assignments indicating that they did not consent to Turnitin.com's use of their work. iParadigms pursued a counterclaim, seeking indemnification against the students' claims, based on a clause in the clickwrap agreement. It also made a separate counterclaim for fraud against one of the students, who in addition to submission of his work for his high school class used Turnitin. com to submit a paper to the University of California, San Diego, employing a student ID that was not his.

The court held for iParadigms, in favor of Turnitin.com, primarily because it decided that the clickwrap agreement was enforceable. The court disallowed that the disclaimer students added to their work had any effect and remarked that the students had the choice to submit their work and agree to Turnitin.com's terms or not submit the work, declaring that there was no duress from iParadigms. The court wrote, "Insofar as Plaintiffs' duress defense is asserted against Plaintiffs' respective schools, rather than Defendant iParadigms, there is no support for the proposition that a contract can be invalidated on the basis of third party duress" (13). The court claimed that even if the students' school was involved, "schools have a right to decide how to monitor and address plagiarism in their schools and may employ companies like iParadigms to help do so" (13).

Beyond support of iParadigms' clickwrap agreement claim, the court also declared that Turnitin.com's was a fair use because it was transformative, meaning that the work was changed significantly to create a new purpose or character from the work, comparing iParadigms' use to precedentially supported use of thumbnails by Google (*Perfect 10 v. Google* 721). Ironically, the court also found that the purpose and character of the students' works were transformed from support of education and creative expression to policing plagiarism and deemed this to be transformative enough to allow it. The court considered the nature and character of the work and decided that iParadigms' use did not hamper the incentive for creativity. And even though Turnitin.com copies students' work in its entirety, the court found that iParadigms was not liable for copyright violation based on the amount and substantiality of the work used, arguing that using a whole work does not automatically preclude a fair use. The court's overall justification for its decision was based in its conclusion that the use provided a benefit to the public.

Beyond these bases for its decision, the court rejected the students' claim that the marketability of their work could be harmed. The court rejected the students' argument that flagging their work in Turnitin.com in relationship to plagiarism, which could mislead readers to assume that their work was plagiaristic, could hamper their opportunities for college entrance, among other detriments. The court rejected this argument, claiming that the harm is speculative and that" [a]nyone who is reasonably familiar with Turnitin's operation will be able to recognize that the identical match is not the result of plagiarism, but simply the result of Plaintiff's earlier submission" (22).

The court denied all of iParadigms' counterclaims and refused to provide it with a damages award or to support its fraud claim.

Regardless of the current case outcome, there are flaws in the court's reasoning that merit appeal, and the *Chronicle of Higher Education* notes the response of the students' attorney: "'I'm definitely appealing,'" said Robert A. Vanderhye, a retired lawyer in Virginia who took on the students' case pro bono. "'I am positive that the appellate court will reverse" on the fair-use issue, he added. The judge, he continued, 'copied'" the company's brief. "'He didn't even consider any of our arguments,' said Mr. Vanderhye" (*Chronicle*). But Peter Jaszi considers that " the judge's argument that the plagiarism tool is covered by fair use because it is transformative may well stand up to an appeal" and notes that if it is upheld, a decision of this kind would be supportive of users like Google, who wish to copy full texts of creators' materials for use in "Google Library" (*Chronicle*).

Several aspects of this case are troubling in regard to questions of students' rights in their work. The court upheld the validity of a clickwrap "agreement" in its finding that students submitted their work without meeting the court's assessment of legal duress, despite students having made clear that they did not intend to permit Turnitin.com's use and that because they were forced to click "I accept" to submit their work actual duress was demonstrated. The court seems to simultaneously disavow the relationship between iParadigms and the schools in declaring that the students agreed to submit their work without duress, based on its conclusion that duress originated from the schools rather than from iParadigms, while at the same time validating the relationship between the schools and iParadigms by treating iParadigms, through Turnitin.com, as an extension of school administrations for purposes of policing student work.

The court further asserts, "If Plaintiffs' objection is that their schools' policies requiring students to use Turnitin are wrongful, Plaintiffs' proper redress is with the school systems" (14). In this court the school administrations had legal power to force students to give up their copyright control to avoid failing in class; but the ethicality of school administrators' use of force is questionable, at best. The students' attempts to retain their copyrights regardless of school mandates makes it clear that they had no power for redress within their institutions, and in this light the court's suggestion implies obvious disregard for students' rights.

In addition, the work that students created was copied in whole and unaltered other than to reproduce it in digital form. Yet the court claims that "the fact that the new work, produced by the defendant, is 'transformative' or 'adds something new, with a further purpose or different character' is strong evidence that the use is a fair use" (15). The court makes no note, however, that the works themselves are not transformed; and although they are used with a further purpose, that new purpose is to generate money for a third party in the process of providing policing instead of the original purpose, to be created as a part of a learning process. In deciding as it did, the court effectively supplanted the students' works' educational purpose with one that is commercial, supporting the business of iParadigms.

The court also dismissed the students' claim that their reputations might be harmed by work that arises within a database flagged for plagiarism, estimating the claim as speculative and stating, "Anyone who is reasonably familiar with Turnitin's operation will be able to recognize that the identical match is not the result of plagiarism, but simply the result of Plaintiff's earlier submission" (22). But the court's assessment of Turnitin's familiarity to the public is itself speculative, and if the assumption does not hold true, it is the students who pay the price for the mistake in assessment.

If this decision is not reversed on appeal, this court will have opened the door for broader use of students' copyrights, both in and out of the Academy by shutting down students' control over the copyrights to their work while in educational systems. And copyrights of all authors may also be affected by a supported decision of this kind. As Jaszi notes, "If this opinion, as it stands, were to be endorsed on appeal, it can only help the cause of Google Library" (now settled; qtd. in Foster). And where this case can hamper students' rights to protect their copyrights, it could arguably pave the way for more freedom to use others' work, if courts rule consistently in favor of all users as this court has ruled for iParadigms. Regardless of the holding in this case, students must always remain aware of the consequences of plagiaristic acts, knowing that whatever means an educational system might use, being caught plagiarizing can lead to a wide range of unpleasant consequences.

Punishment for Plagiarism

In cases where evidence mounts against those students who are most likely guilty of plagiarism, they often face uncertain futures because there is no consistent structure among institutions for treating violations. As one author notes, "One of the most striking characteristics of plagiarism is that its investigation, adjudication, and punishment are typically committed to educational and professional institutions that resolve the charges, essentially, in private" (Green 199). There are a range of responses to plagiarism, but the list below notes those which are most typical:

Sanctions against plagiarism include

(1) grade reduction
(2) rejection of paper or exam; failing grade for assignment or course
(3) reprimand
(4) temporary or permanent disqualification from employment or academic program
(5) suspension
(6) expulsion or dismissal

(Thomas 429)

These sanctions indicate a broad range of potential penalties; students often have no notice beforehand of which penalty will be applied, and they often have no option to influence the use of one penalty over another. While students certainly should not be allowed to plagiarize and should be punished for their violations, those who are sanctioned more severely than others may find themselves unfairly disadvantaged. Institutions that maintain clear policies about determination of plagiarism, as well as guidelines for choosing sanctions, also create more opportunity to ensure that their students are treated ethically.

It is clear that ethical consideration of choices for treating intellectual products in academic settings is important for students, professors, and administrators alike. And educational institutions could be the ideal venue for students not only to gain intellectual understanding of ethical considerations to avoid punishment but also to develop a sense of personal ethics that could lead them to make ethical choices in their work both inside and outside the academy. Professors, as well, could consider ethical choices as a basis for course and class management, and might find that they can incorporate treatment of ethics as part of course content. In addition, they might examine the relationship of pedagogical choice to students' actions regarding their courses of study. Pedagogical choices can play a large role in how students are perceived and how they perceive themselves as creators. So this issue and its significance, as well as ethics, are treated in detail in the conclusion.

Conclusion: Legal, Ethical, and Pedagogical Considerations

Both educators and their students have ethical duties regarding how they use intellectual products. Both have ethical duties to use creative products with concern for their creators or controllers, students have ethical duties to treat educators' and their institutions' intellectual products with respect, and educators and educational institutions have a special—fiduciary—duty to handle students' work, their experience on campuses, and their training with care. And in cases where students can substantiate unethical treatment of their work by professors, they may be able to resort to a new development in the law by claiming breach of fiduciary duty (Astala 33). To substantiate a claim of breach of fiduciary duty, a student must show a close relationship with the professor, in which she or he relied on the professor for help, advice, or support, determined by means of consideration of a variety of factors including the degree of affinity between them; differences in age, health, mental abilities, education, and business experience; and the extent of trust elicited from the student (34).

In addition to Joany Chou's success in her claim in *Chou v. Univ. of Chicago*, discussed in chapter 1, others' claims of breach of fiduciary duty have been supported by courts in holdings as well as in dicta (*Rainey v. Wayne State Univ., Johnson v. Schmidt*). In claims of breach of fiduciary duty, the focus is on poor judgment of a professor, but many other rights and responsibilities attached to educators and students are the same or similar. Differences arise because students and educators may interact with responsibilities under different contextual parameters. These are noted and discussed below, treating students' rights and responsibilities first, educators' next, and the interaction of the two, last.

Students' Ethical and Legal Responsibilities

With students' rights come responsibilities as participants in a democratic society, and these responsibilities include ethical responses to using intellectual products created by others. Students represent themselves not only by the work they create but by the uses they make of others' work. They represent themselves and display integrity through attribution to sources they use in the work they develop; they represent their credibility and authority through effective use of sources as support for ideas, argument, and creative thought processes developed in the process of learning; and they represent a legal stance in the ways they use work that is protected under intellectual property law.

Students who seek respect for the work they create must respond to other creators' works with respect if they expect their professors and other users to show consideration to theirs. Their experience with intellectual products in educational settings forms the basis for finding the balance between intellectual product use and protection that is necessary to uphold constitutional intent of the intellectual property provision. Finding this balance can be difficult for students in technical communication and fields like it as they prepare for workplace authorship practices in which single-sourced work (materials developed by a team) and collaborative authorship are common.

After finding that technical communication textbooks likened plagiarism to theft and stated that using the Internet leads to plagiarism, one author wrote that students in technical communication are sent a too stringent message (Reyman 62–63). But assimilating understanding of balance is part of the imprinting process that shapes students' perceptions of law and society. Learning to interact ethically with intellectual products also is necessary for students to understand how their interactions in society affect the way both the law and society itself are shaped. The Supreme Court supports dialogic interaction on campuses and makes clear that campuses act, in essence, as training grounds for new citizens who will shape the nation in the future. The Court notes that universities play a "vital role in a democracy" by enabling a "robust exchange of ideas" that allows its inhabitants to discover truth "out of a multitude of tongues," "making the university a 'marketplace of ideas'" (*Keyishian v. Bd. of Regents*).

Through their intellectual interactions, students are learning that they do and will affect the shape of the country, so understanding how to maintain balance is a particularly important and essential part of their education. Students learn to treat intellectual products in three general areas: attribution to avoid plagiarism, citation in support of their own concepts and arguments, and ethical and legal use of protected intellectual materials. These treatments are discussed below, in turn.

Student Attribution to Avoid Plagiarism

Plagiarism and students' rights are discussed at length in the fourth chapter, but the other side of the coin focuses on students' responsibilities to avoid plagiarism. Some note that plagiarism detection services can be ineffectual for locating students' plagiarism (McMillan 6). One reporter found, for instance, that tests of Turnitin.com's software concluded that it does not work well. He notes that a physics professor found that when he submitted his students' papers for plagiarism detection, the files to which the detection service pointed as those which were copied rendered "404 file not found" errors, leading the professor to question how students might plagiarize files that did not exist.

To examine the service further, the professor created his own purposely "plagiarized" paper containing verbatim copied material from several prominent journals, to find that in this case, the software did not detect plagiarism (MacMillan 6). Law professor Dan Burk also notes that using plagiarism detection "promotes a climate of mistrust between students, teachers, and administrators" (6), which, of course, leads to unhealthy learning environments.

More important than the problems with policing plagiarism in attempts to eliminate it is that taking a combative stance reduces treatment of plagiarism to a policing effort rather than providing learning instances. Deepening the offense, students who use plagiarism as a shortcut hinder their learning experiences and reinforce bad habits that can impair their effectiveness in their posteducational futures. Students also must consider that their choices whether or not to plagiarize represent who they are as people and that lack of respect and poor reputation, which may seem meaningless to them while they rush through their college experiences, can revisit them in the future.

Using Attribution for Authority and Credibility

Beyond citing others' work to avoid plagiarism, there is strong rationale supporting students' source attribution to create credibility and authority in their own work. Students who learn that citing sources is not only a tedious task that they must complete to meet course requirements, or "to follow the rules" but is also a means to provide and support content for their ideas, arguments, and explanations of their developed or developing new concepts may begin to understand attribution in a new way. Students who realize that using attribution is a way to enter the textual conversation of their disciplines are able to see their work as more meaningful and see themselves as authors who can interact with authority and truly participate in academic interchange. This characterization of their work is a far cry from that of merely creating rote products in response to meaningless class assignments.

Legal and Ethical Use of Intellectual Products

It is possible for a student (or professor) to use an intellectual product in a way that plagiarizes but does not violate copyright. And it is possible to use a product in a way that infringes copyright but does not plagiarize. Students who understand the differences and make choices that are consistent with their intended uses have advantages over those who do not. When students use sources that are in the public domain and not copyrighted but reproduce the materials verbatim and fail to attribute them, they would be at fault for plagiarism but not for copyright violation. The offense in this case would be that students misrepresented themselves as authors of works that they did not create; in doing so, they would have failed to complete their assigned work. They also would have violated actual authors' rights to represent themselves through their work. So students wrong themselves by not going through learning experiences in the process of creating works, and they wrong actual authors in the process. Violations in this case are mostly ethical, but some argue that even legal arguments of violation might apply. Ethical issues involve the lie of misrepresentation and the disregard for authors' efforts and self-representation—their credibility and authority in the work that they have created.

Even though in a literal sense U.S. law is based on statute, long after the law of equity was abolished, the European Union's "moral rights" argument is still sometimes used to argue in favor of personal rights in creators to protect the works they develop. But "[l]egislators repeatedly declined to enact moral-rights legislation, and courts disavowed moral rights as a part of copyright law" (Stearns 531; see *Gilliam v. American Broadcasting Cos.*, 538 F.2d 14, 24 [2d Cir. 1976]) As one author notes, "American copyright law, as presently written, does not recognize moral rights or provide a cause of action for their violation, since the law seeks to vindicate the economic rather than the personal rights of authors" (Stearns 531). So students must make clear distinctions between how their uses of others' material will be treated under ethical standards or under the law.

Students violate copyright without committing plagiarism when they make a copy of or use a protected source without permission and without a right in fair use, free speech, or personal use. For instance, where, without permission, students decorate their publicly accessible Web sites with images that they did not create, they violate copyright, even when the images are used only for decoration and they provide attribution to the creator of the images. In cases like these, their attribution negates the potential for plagiarism and ensures that viewers make no mistake in authorship, but students' unlicensed and unexcused use of the images infringes the copyrights of the creators. Where students' ethicality might come into question for embellishing their sites with others' work rather than making the effort to create embellishment of their own, the legal violation of copyright in this case could be more serious.

Reconceptualizing Authorship, Attribution, and Copyright

Digitalization is affecting how society perceives authorship, attribution, and copyright law, and neither legislators nor most in academe have paced with a non-Romantic, poststructural, deconstructed view of authorship and the different ways that authority is construed in a digital world. Students, many of whom were born after the advent of the Internet and grew up using computer-mediated communication and Web-based information gathering, take for granted the effects of hypertextual mixing of sources, ideas, authorship, and comment into final products in which exact authorship, authority, and power are hard to place. Coupled with the potential, even likelihood, that these products will change and evolve in a nonstatic dance of interactive reconfiguration, attribution of authorship and authority is beginning to become less meaningful.

As a matter of course, e-mail posts embed the commentaries of all the posters who have come before, and blogs include comment, images, and video provided by various, often anonymous contributors. The cut-and-paste process of moving text around, reincorporating it into different formats, and synthesizing and resynthesizing it to create new expressions is common in the digital world. As academic responses to textual works support intellectual dialogue, recontextualization of text, images, sound, and video on the Internet provides digital dialogue for the wired community. Grabbing digital information and splashing it onto venues such as YouTube is becoming a common form of public dialogue, and interaction with bits and pieces of digitized material allows average individuals to make political statements, report news, make public commentary, and create parody in a way that connects people from different areas of the country (and the world) in a way that has never been possible before. That the processes of finding, copying, and posting materials of all kinds is becoming common indicates a shift in how society values information and its authorship. Students are front runners in the move into the digital future, and their attitudes often reflect a minimized attribution of power and authority to authorship. At a time when even the potential to attribute authorship has declined, the concepts that drive attachment of power to authorship have weakened. Students readily accept that

> all of a person's ideas and expressions are composites of the person's exposure to the ideas and expressions of others, as comprehended by and melded with the person's own ideas and expressions. Some ideas and expressions have become so widespread and familiar that they have permeated into a sort of public domain, immune to creative or proprietary claims of anyone and available for use by all. (Thomas 422)

Digitization is changing the way we value authorship and the authority that accompanies it, but the law and the literary-philosophical viewpoint common to many educators has not always changed with it. In fact, the potential for broad worldwide access to available information and the technological ease and exactitude with which the global public can send and reach information threaten not only those who benefit from controlling information but also the traditional, Romantic treatment of authorship in which many educators are still invested. Some of this investment appears in the pedagogical choices that educators make, which focus on providing students with information as authority that they are encouraged to embrace merely because their professors want them to. Below, a discussion of pedagogical strategy for dealing with plagiarism and treating protected intellectual products examines the impact that pedagogical choice can have in tackling problematic aspects.

Students must also consider that even though attitudes toward authorship and authority that derive from effects of digitization and hypertextual source mixing may be moving our culture in new directions, acceptance of unattributed and unlicensed use not supported by fair use or personal use does not yet universally follow. The strictures that guide their actions when they use other creators' sources may not allow uses that they assume are supported. Just as the Constitution requires a balance between the public's right to access authored material and an author's need to benefit from it, there is also a necessary balance between actions that contribute to societal change and the need to adhere to extant law. There is no bright-line indica-tor of where that balance is, so students have to make good-faith efforts in use and in the way they go about creating change. Making changes with a concern for ethics is more effective, and students can choose to represent themselves well if they consider ethics in the ways they effect change.

Ideally, educators could take advantage of changes in cultural attitudes toward authorship, authority, and control of information to educate stu-dents about ways to treat these issues within their distinct disciplines, particularly since different disciplines consider them in different ways. Addressing plagiarism, copyright, and patent treatment is important to students today, regardless of their field of study, and examining these is-sues rounds out their educations. Both students and their professors have ethical duties to the creators of intellectual products, but educators have a particular responsibility, a fiduciary duty of care to the students over whom they have power.

Educators' Ethical Duty to Students

Fiduciary duties arise in special relationships that require a level of trust, particularly when trust is required because one party to the relationship has power over another. Educators and academic institutions owe that special fiduciary duty to students because they have a broad level of control over students' achievements while in their institutions. And because stu-dents rely on professors and administrators to provide honest assessment of their work in the forms of grades and recommendations for employment or graduate school, instructors have an ethical duty to be particularly care-ful of the effect they have on students' futures. The imbalance in power between students and those in authority in their educational institutions makes it likely that students would hesitate to demand their rights of au-thorship in copyrighted products, and as previous chapters in this book have described, the potential for ethical violation or infringement of student work in a variety of areas is high. Students should be credited for work they contribute to patent development (see Chou), and for nonpatentable work they should be credited both in copyright control and forms of at-tribution consistent with literary-philosophical concepts of authorship; in articles, essays, software, videos, music, scientific papers, and other kinds of intellectual products created among various units of academic inter-est, students maintain the same rights as do other creators under the law.

In addition, administrators and instructors should not attempt to treat students' intellectual products as works for hire unless the students who created them were actual employees and working within the scope of their duties. Clearly, a misuse of power to coerce students' compliance with use of their work against their wishes would go beyond what an ethical duty, arising from the relationship, would allow. Instructors should inhibit the potential to take advantage of student vulnerability by avoiding use of student contributions in unethical ways. Professors' stories of lack of ethics among faculty colleagues are, unfortunately, not as uncommon as they should be. One interviewee, a former professor at a large state university, noted that in the case of several students outside his discipline whom he happened to know well, it was considered a common occurrence for professors to use student article contributions without attribution (Anonymous2).

Educators generally police themselves in their interactions with students and their work, but when students violate their own ethical duties to authors, their commitments to class processes, or legal prohibition against misuse of others' legally protected work, the burden to deal with the problems that result most often fall on educators' shoulders.

Student Copyright Infringement

P2P

Students may be characterized most broadly not as copyright holders but as infringers in relation to copyright law as a result of *A&M records v. Napster* (discussed in chapter 3), which focused on the large numbers of university students accused of sharing copyright-protected music files. And battles against student file sharing rage on (also discussed in detail in chapter 3). But beyond the legal ramifications, ethical considerations arise for both students and their educational institutions. As discussed in chapter 3, file sharing goes beyond legal issues: students and others believe that big business is unfairly overwhelming markets for musical expression, and many employ file sharing as a means of civil disobedience of sorts. Beyond arguments regarding personal decisions to effect change by using extralegal methods, students must consider the ethical ramifications of file sharing on campus, using university Internet service providers (ISPs) as their means to engage, potentially, in infringing behavior. Not all file sharing is infringing, of course, and a number of contexts allow legal file sharing that can be particularly supportive of educational activitIt is not yet clear whether a university ISP can be held accountable for the actions of its students under the DMCA (*Grokster*), but university providers have had to pay for legal defenses in claims against them and one could potentially be held liable. From an ethical standpoint, students should consider their actions carefully at the point of engaging in file sharing. If they copy and distribute copyright-protected materials and have no clear right in fair use or personal use to do so, they put their institutions at risk. Students must realize that university equipment and services are provided to support the educational process rather than to entertain. Where education and entertainment come together, it is often difficult to determine the limits of appropriate activity and use of university technology, and students must make best judgments in acting ethically within their educational institutions.

Web and Blog Inclusions

Students also have ethical and legal responsibilities regarding the materials they use on Web sites and blogs. Just like any other situation in which students must be careful not to infringe copyrights, they must maintain care to use copyrighted materials appropriately on the Internet. Where personal and fair use protects users from infringement when copying and responding to copyrighted materials in some cases, not all use of materials is supported. And when students load copyrighted materials to globally accessible Internet sites, they run a higher risk of violation, so they have an added duty of care to consider the legal ramifications of their uses carefully. (See more detailed discussion in chapter 3.) In addition, from an ethical standpoint, students should consider that in light of their association with their universities, they represent their institutions. Students should be aware not only that their actions could lead to legal liability for their institutions but that they might also affect their institutions' reputations.

Students should also be careful not to use university server space as a means to engage in activities that might not be legally supported and whose legal responsibility could be assigned to the university. For instance, students who consider creating new software to develop their own P2P file-sharing service, loading it to university servers, and making it available for file sharing, even if they intend to share materials in the public domain or intend the structure to be used for sharing materials supported by personal or fair use, should work with their institutions to gain approval to avoid both legal and ethical conflicts.

Student Plagiarism

Treated in detail in chapter 4, the rise in student plagiarism is haunting instructors and academic administrators, and many have called for what some might consider exacting solutions. But dealing with student plagiarism is problematic. It is harmful to academic institutions because it can engender a negative reputation for the department or school affected. Unpunished plagiarism also allows some students to claim credit they do not deserve, in addition to harming those whose work is plagiarized. As chapter 4 details, using plagiarism detection services can be a poor solution because services can be ineffectual, they can be unethical, they can create bad learning environments, and they can violate students' copyrights. Those who have studied the problem at length suggest a range of ways to defeat it. But there are difficulties. "[I]t is not always easy to distinguish between writing that is copied with the intent of being passed off as the plagiarist's own and writing that is merely subject to the inadvertent 'influence' of earlier work" (Green 171). And students who are learning to make distinctions between others' work and their own have particular difficulty making distinctions. One author makes clear how it might be possible to confuse authorship:

> Some thinkers have conceived of art as essentially imitative. Stories that depict common experiences or illuminate life's dilemmas are told and retold in myth, poetry, and drama. Creators draw upon the works of their predecessors and offer up their own works for the use and enjoyment of others. Given this interdependence of human creative efforts, requirements of complete originality or novelty become difficult, if not impossible, to impose in evaluating the success or value of a literary work. The idea of plagiarism is thus something of a paradox. Why condemn an author for borrowing from another if such borrowing is inevitable and even fundamental to the creative process? The answer lies in the kind of borrowing an author does. (Stearns 516)

To add to the complexity of this problem, "[m]any influences are unconscious. An idea, phrase, argument, melody, or insight read or heard long ago can lodge in the unconscious" (Green 180). So educators have an important duty to help students distinguish between acts that could be considered plagiarism and those that most likely could not.

Even under the best of circumstances, some students may still engage in plagiarism. Propositions for responding to students' plagiarism include suggestions that "writing instructors develop a stronger understanding of students' approaches to tasks and the invitation that we trust students' understandings of responsibility and authorship" (Kolich [1983] in DeVoss and Rosati 195). Likewise, we should "share with students definitions of academic honesty and cases of plagiarism to enable students to read, analyze, and understand institutional approaches to academic honesty" (Hawley [1984], Whitacker [1993], and Wilhoit [1994] in DeVoss and Rosati 197). In attempts to allay student use of paper mills, "some professors started using more in-class writing assignments and other professors shifted from term-papers to final examinations. Some refused to accept photocopies of papers. Others started requiring conferences, interim assignments, and other drafts before the final paper was due. Still others required a series of shorter writing assignments throughout the semester so the professor could become familiar with each student's writing style" (Dickerson 32–33). Another suggests that "building strong rhetorical purpose into our assignments allows students to have a much more clear focus when they begin their work" (DeVoss and Rosati). In addition, some note that "[f]ocusing on microtasks and task management is another approach to encouraging students to better understand and manage a complex assignment and deter them from plagiarism" (Kantz [1990] and Kloss [1996] in DeVoss and Rosati).

Traditional Pedagogy and the Treatment of Students' Work

Traditional pedagogy focuses on transferring information from an instructor or some other form of authority, such as a well-supported book or journal, directly to students as receptacles for knowledge. The assumption is that the source of authority can provide "correct" answers or information that must be considered fact or "Truth." Commonly, traditional classes follow a pattern in which the instructor lectures to the class members, rarely if ever asking for responses or discussion from student participants. Traditional pedagogy strongly supports a Romantic conceptualization of authorship because it focuses class interaction on the authority of those already in power positions. The nature of this conceptual treatment devalues students' work by way of their lack of status, where, under a Romantic characterization, they would not be considered authors. Concepts that drive traditional pedagogy can allow those who are unaware of its impact to treat student work as if it has no authorship, thus making violation of copyright in the work seem minimally harmful, if at all.

In addition, traditional pedagogy can emphasize the instructor's knowledge and power, forcing students to accept blindly that whatever the instructor tells them is truth. The problems with this process are severalfold. It allows memorization rather than learning, it creates unquestioning students, it focuses attention on the instructor's interests rather than students', it assumes that students have nothing of value to offer to the learning process, it bores students, and it allows them to denigrate the educational process as valueless other than for obtaining a degree. One author notes that "too many students—and sometimes their parents—are more concerned about getting a certain degree. . . . They view a 'college' education as a mere commodity, as a ticket that has to be punched on their way to a career in corporate America" (Dickerson 24).

Traditional pedagogy also places all power and responsibility for learning in the hands of the instructor, and it minimizes the potential for students and instructors to develop together new knowledge based on a synthesis of all their ideas, research, and creative efforts. When students fail to value their own work and devalue the educational process as nothing more than a means to obtain the degree, the likelihood is greater that they will take shortcuts to completing assignments. As such, traditional pedagogy can encourage plagiarism rather than hamper it, not because it justifies cheating but because it may make cheating seem reasonable under the circumstances.

While instructors are usually zealous about the subjects they teach because they choose their areas of specialization and spend countless hours researching, writing, thinking about, and discussing their work, their students may take these instructors' courses only because they have to. With no real desire to engage in the material, students who have no choice but to sit through classes and produce the required assignments to receive passing grades are more likely to take shortcuts. A system that requires instructors to force students to engage in developing work in which they have no interest tends to pit instructors and students against each other. And when students try to bypass the work in which they have no interest by plagiarizing, instructors and administrators then, by necessity, engage in policing activities, further setting educators and students in opposition to each other.

By the same token, students and educators can enter conflict relationships when instructors or administrators copy or distribute students' work without a license or fail to attribute their contributions to patents or scientific research. Ideally, instructors and students would work together to further students' educational development.

Practical Pedagogical Strategies for Avoiding Plagiarism and Copyright Violation

Pinpointing a problem is helpful, but solutions are more difficult to create and employ. Those submitted here are primarily pedagogical. Ideally, students and professors would focus their efforts jointly, not just in support of memorizing information or remembering what a professor had to say but also on the process of supporting students in efforts to learn how to learn. Successful learning environments produce students who perceive their activities in academia as meaningful and see that the communicative work they create is a means to being included in the conversation of the fields they study. And students who learn well understand that the sources they use in their work allow them to gather authority for the ideas that represent them as new participants in their educational environments and in the disciplines they enter. Students who understand that respect can come from participating in real communicative interaction in their fields would be less likely to plagiarize because they grasp the value of creating work without it. The fostering of learning environments that focus on student's creative thinking, communicating, and interacting would provide more effective deterrents to plagiarism than the employment of detection services that merely allow educators to catch students who copy work to avoid completing assignments in which they see no value.

Students whose work is treated with respect and who are treated like authors who create work of real value, assigned with rights and duties like all other authors, are more likely to see themselves as integrated into a system in which requirements for use and creation of work are a part of the price of entry. In addition, students who see themselves as real authors are more likely to respect the authorship of others and to make fair use of copyrighted work as a way to integrate and interact with ideas. They have the opportunity to experience the value both of use and of the need to protect work. This background is particularly important since these students will be shaping the direction of intellectual property law in the future, both by culturally influencing how law is interpreted and, as creators and users who are directly subject to its powers, by demanding change in law. Educators who take steps to make clear that students' work has value and help students see the value in their work could go a long way toward inhibiting plagiarism, as well as becoming less likely to assume that it can be used without permission.

Practical strategies for accomplishing the goals noted above require a shift away from traditional pedagogy. Technical communication journals are filled with works that forward a social constructionist basis for pedagogy (the social perspective). Among a list too long to count are books and articles by Cargile Cook, Cargile Cook and Grant-Davie, Lipson and Day, Thralls and Blyler, Whithaus and Magnotto Neff, and Savage. These works, among the many others that reflect pedagogical thought in the technical communication field, are vast in perspective but consistent in noting different aspects of importance in teaching with pedagogy that focuses on student responsibility, creativity, and their ethical treatment as authors.

A learning environment that focuses on students' ideas and authorship of original thought would ideally be based on abolishing grades altogether. The professor would have little power over students' actions; they could choose to come to class to learn, motivated by perceptions of class activities as beneficial; and students would produce their work with a true desire to learn and to enter the conversation of their fields. Of course, this utopian possibility has pragmatic limitations that would likely not be overcome in most practical applications. But less radical alternatives could be effective in helping students learn useful ways to interact with and produce new knowledge.

Genuine authorship comes when students create new work for a real purpose. Fred Kemp made this clear in the 1980s when he networked twenty Apple computers and asked his first-year composition students at the University of Texas to write to each other about issues that moved them rather than writing essays that only their instructor would read. Others followed suit and found that students who wrote about issues over which they were genuinely concerned, and who communicated their concerns to each other, were more engaged in writing processes, developed better-supported communication projects and were more motivated to work through learning processes. Years of research that followed have highlighted both negative and positive aspects of these early experiments with computer-based composition instruction, but overall, the premise that real engagement in authentic learning practices is more effective for supporting student authorship holds true.

Following early entry into computer-based pedagogy, projects have been developed that employ even more genuine uses for networked technology to create authentic communication situations. The Global Classroom Project is one of these, creating a forum for experiential learning in technical communication. The Project requires students in Russia and America to collaborate over the Internet to develop joint analytical reports regarding issues in comparative cross-cultural communication (Herrington "Where in the World"; Herrington and Tretyakov). Other new means to develop genuine learning environments include service projects in which students create documents and special research for nonprofit organizations (Sapp and Crabtree; Ornatowski and Bekins). In these kinds of learning experiences, students focus on developing work within non-class-based circumstances in which the work they develop is unique and often creative. Students are able to develop intellectual products in situations in which their authorship has to be original because it must meet the contextual needs of the specific projects with which they work. These kinds of learning situations require broad preparation from the professors who offer them, and they can be difficult to arrange and time-consuming for all involved. But smaller-scale learning endeavors that focus on genuine student authorship are possible even in more traditional class settings.

Students who are required to create work in developmental stages would have a difficult time plagiarizing works unless they refuse to submit drafts as required, and if they follow the required pattern, they would be more likely to understand the differing incremental steps in creating new work as they struggle through the stages. For instance, students might be required to write proposals for final projects at the beginning of a term, then develop midterm progress reports to assess the work they have completed up to that point. They might be required to present the material in their projects and explain each aspect of the work, and then, finally, submit the final project as a culmination of each stage. Every assignment in the project could also be developed in drafting stages so that students could improve on each draft throughout the development process. Students who submit drafts and create work in stages have to work very hard to plagiarize such assignments. They might instead develop pride in taking responsibility for their work that comes with authorship, claimed as their own.

More important is that students might also begin to see themselves as authors whose work represents who they are and what they have to offer. They might also begin to see themselves as participants in a broader enterprise than the educational process and want to try on their roles as citizens in the realm of democratic interaction. Ultimately, as is the case with all other participants in democracy, students can only be supported in the rights it confers when they assume the responsibilities that sustain those rights. An educational structure that supports students' rights in their work can provide a basis for encouraging the very enterprise that the Supreme Court supported in *Keyishian v. Board of Regents*:

> Our Nation is deeply committed to safeguarding academic freedom, which is of transcendent value to all of us and not merely to the teachers concerned. That freedom is therefore a special concern of the First Amendment, which does not tolerate laws that cast a pall of orthodoxy over the classroom. "The vigilant protection of constitutional freedoms is nowhere more vital than in the community of American schools." *Shelton v. Tucker, supra,* at 487. The classroom is peculiarly the "marketplace of ideas." The Nation's future depends upon leaders trained through wide exposure to that robust exchange of ideas which discovers truth "out of a multitude of tongues, [rather] than through any kind of authoritative selection." *United States v. Associated Press,* 52 F.Supp. 362, 372. In *Sweezy v. New Hampshire,* 354 U.S. 234, 250, we said:

The essentiality of freedom in the community of American universities is almost self-evident. No one should underestimate the vital role in a democracy that is played by those who guide and train our youth. To impose any strait jacket upon the intellectual leaders in our colleges and universities would imperil the future of our Nation. No field of education is so thoroughly comprehended by man that new discoveries cannot yet be made. Particularly is that true in the social sciences, where few, if any, principles are accepted as absolutes. Scholarship cannot flourish in an atmosphere of suspicion and distrust. Teachers and students must always remain free to inquire, to study and to evaluate, to gain new maturity and understanding; otherwise our civilization will stagnate and die.

My hope is that students will begin not only to understand the importance of their rights to use intellectual products as a means to support democratic endeavor but also to engage in the democratic enterprise ethically and legally, cognizant that with rights come responsibilities. And that when they take on the mantle of responsibilities from those who teach them, they will do so prepared to support a strong and robust structure of democracy, fair use, and free speech that reflects the values that make a democratic nation one of which its citizens can be proud.

Works Cited and Consulted

Index

Works Cited and Consulted

A&M Records, Inc. v. Napster, Inc. 2001 U.S. Dist. LEXIS 2186 (N.D. Cal. Mar. 5, 2001), aff'd, 284 F.3d 1091 (9th Cir. 2002).

American Library Association. Copyright. Web. May 29, 2007 <http://www.ala.org/ala/washoff/woissues/copyrightb/copyright.cfm>; later changed to <http://www.ala.org/ala/issuesadvocacy/copyright/index.cfm>.

Anonymous. Personal interview. Java Monkey Cafe, Decatur, GA. May 27, 2007.

Anonymous2. Telephone interview. May 26, 2007.

Apple Computer, Inc. v. Franklin Computer Corp., 714 F.2d 1240, 1252 (3d Cir. 1983).

Astala, Melissa. "Wronged by a Professor? Breach of Fiduciary Duty as a Remedy in Intellectual Property Infringement Cases. 3 *Houston Business and Tax Law Journal* 31. 31–63.

A.V. et al. v. iParadigms, Limited Liability Company. Civ. Act. no. 07-0293 (E.D. Va., March 11, 2008).

Axberg, Robyn. "File-Sharing Tools and Copyright Law: A Study of In re Aimster Copyright Litigation and MGM Studios, Inc. v. Grokster, Ltd." 35 *Loyola University Chicago Law Journal* 389 (2003). 389–455.

Baker (Graham), Margaret Ann, and Carol David. "The Rhetoric of Power: Political Issues in Management Writing." *Technical Communication Quarterly* 3 (1994): 165–78.

Bathaee, Yavar. "A Constitutional Idea-Expression Doctrine: Qualifying Congress' Commerce Power When Protecting Intellectual Property Right." 18 *Fordham Intellectual Property Media and Entertainment Law Journal* 441 (2008). 441–513.

Bill Graham Archives v. Dorling Kindersley, Ltd. 448 F.3d 605 (2d Cir. 2006).

Bushnell, Jack. "A Contrary View of the Technical Writing Classroom: Notes toward Future Discussion." *Technical Communication Quarterly* 8 (1999): 175–88.

Byrne v. BBC. 132 F. Supp. 2d 229 (S.D.N.Y. 2001).

Campbell v. Acuff-Rose Music. 510 U.S. 569 (1994).

Cargile Cook, Kelli. "Layered Literacies: A Theoretical Frame for Technical Communication Pedagogy." *Technical Communication Quarterly* 11 (2002): 5–29.

Cargile Cook, Kelli, and Keith Grant-Davie, eds. *Online Education: Global Questions, Local Answers.* Amityville, NY: Baywood, 2005.

Carr v. Signa Securities, Inc. 93 F.3d, 944.

C.C.N.V. v. Reid. 490 U.S. 730 (1989).

Chou v. University of Chicago. 254 F.3d (Fed. Cir. 2001).

Cohn, Cindy. "*Felten v. RIAA* Case Overview and Outline." From EFF Press Conference for *Felten v. RIAA.* June 6, 2001, San Francisco, CA. Web. June 23, 2007. <http://radio.eff.org/radio_shows/pc1.mp3>.

"Combating Internet Piracy on College Campuses." Capitol Hill Hearing. House Education and Workforce Committee. Subcommittee, 21st Century Competitiveness. Testimony by Dan Glickman, CEO, Motion Picture Association of America. *Congressional Quarterly, Inc.* Sept. 26, 2006.

Coombe, Rosemary. *The Cultural Life of Intellectual Properties: Authorship, Appropriation, and the Law.* Durham: Duke UP, 1998.

Copyright Management Center. Distance Education. Indiana University, Purdue University, Indianapolis. Web. April 2003; June 19, 2007. <http://www.copyright.iupui.edu/dist_learning.htm>.

Copyright Term Extension Act. 17 U.S.C. §§108, 203, 301–4.

DeVoss, Danielle, and A. C. Rosati. "It Wasn't Me, Was It? Plagiarism and the Web." *Computers and Composition* 19.2 (2002): 191–203.

DeVoss, Nicole, and James E. Porter. "Why Napster Matters to Writing: Filesharing as a New Ethic of Digital Delivery." *Computers and Composition* 23.2 (2006): 178–210.

Diamond v. Diehr. 450 U.S. 175 (1981).

Diaz, Charlsye Smith. "The Technical Writer's Role in Preserving Intellectual Property Rights outside the United States." *IEEE Transactions on Professional Communication* 50.2 (2007): 121–29.

Dickerson, Darby. "Facilitated Plagiarism: The Saga of Term-Paper Mills and the Failure of Legislation and Litigation to Control Them." 52 *Villanova Law Review* 21 (2007). 21–66.

Digital Millennium Copyright Act. Pub. L. No. 105–304, 112 Stat. 2860 (1998).

Ding, Dan. "Marxism, Ideology, Power and Scientific and Technical Writing." *Journal of Technical Writing and Communication* 28.2 (1998): 133–61.

"Disney Finds Copyrights No Mickey Mouse Issue." *Daily News of Los Angeles.* May 2, 1989.

Dorfman, Ariel, and Armand Mattelart. *How to Read Donald Duck: Imperialist Ideology in the Disney Comic.* 2nd ed. New York: International General Pub., 1984.

Dubinsky, James M. *Teaching Technical Communication: Critical Issues for the Classroom.* New York: Bedford/St. Martin's, 2004.

Durack, Katherine T. "Technology Transfer and Patents: Implications for the Production of Scientific Knowledge." *Technical Communication Quarterly* 15 (2006): 315–29.

EFF. "Felten et. al. v. RIAA et. al." Web. Aug. 7, 2002; Apr. 23, 2007. <http://www.eff.org/IP/DMCA/Felten_v_RIAA/>.

———. "Felten v. RIAA Audio Files." Web. June 28, 2007. <http://w2.eff.org/IP/DMCA/Felten_v_RIAA/felten_audio.html>.

Electronic Frontier Foundation. "*JibJab Media v. Ludlow Music* ('This Land' Parody)." *Our Work: Cases.* Web. May 28, 2007. <http://www.eff.org/legal/cases/JibJab_v_Ludlow/>.

Exemption to Prohibition on Circumvention of Copyright Protection Systems for Access Control Technologies. Library of Congress. Copyright Office. 37 CFR Part

201. Docket # RM 2005–11. Web. Jan. 19, 2009. <http://www.copyright.gov/1201/docs/fedreg_notice.pdf>.

Finding Nemo. Walt Disney Pictures, 2003. Film.

Florida, Richard. *The Flight of the Creative Class.* New York: Collins, 2007.

Foucault, Michel. "What Is an Author?" Trans. Donald E. Bouchard and Sherry Simon. In *Language, Counter-Memory, Practice.* Ed. Donald Bouchard. Ithaca, NY: Cornell UP, 1977. 124–27.

Foster, Andrea L. "Plagiarism Detection Tool Creates Legal Quandary." *Chronicle of Higher Education,* May 17, 2002: a37.

Frank, Steven J. "Patent Reform Cacophony." Web. Jan. 17, 2009. <http://www.spectrum.ieee.org/dec05/2349>.

Full Sail v. Spevak. Case no. 6:03-cv-887-ORL-31JGG. Web. Jan. 13, 2009. <http://euro.ecom.cmu.edu/program/law/08–732/DomainNames/FullSailVSpevackDistrict-Court.pdf>.

Funk Bros. Seed Co. v. Kalo Inoculant Co., 333 U.S. 127, 130 (1948).

Gassaway, Laura. "Values Conflict in the Digital Environment: Librarians versus Copyright Holders." *Columbia Journal of Law and the Arts* 24.15 (2000): 115–60.

Gattis, Lyn. F. "Openness, Secrecy, Authorship: Technical Arts and the Culture of Knowledge from Antiquity to the Renaissance." *Technical Communication Quarterly* 13 (2004): 238–40.

Georgia Tech Research Corporation. Office of Technology Licensing. "Policies." Web. May 25, 2007. <http://otl.gtrc.gatech.edu/sect/inventors/faqs#equity>.

Gerdy, Kristin. "Law Student Plagiarism: Why It Happens, Where It's Found, and How to Find It." 2004 *Brigham Young Education and Law Journal* 431 (2004). 431–40.

Giesler, Cheryl, et al. "Future Directions for Research on the Relationship between Information Technology and Writing." *Journal of Business and Technical Communication* 15.3 (2001): 269–309.

Glod, Maria. "McLean Students Sue Anti-Cheating Service." *Washington Post.* Web. Apr. 5, 2007. <http://www.washingtonpost.com/wp-dyn/content/article/2007/03/28/AR2007032802038.html.> Accessed April 5, 2007.

Gottschalk v. Benson, 409 U.S. 63, 67 (1972).

Green, Stuart P. "Plagiarisms, Norms, and the Limits of Theft Law: Some Observations on the Use of Criminal Sanctions in Enforcing Intellectual Property Rights." 54 *Hastings Law Journal* 167 (2002). 169–232.

Gurak, Laura J. *Cyberliteracy: Navigating the Internet with Awareness.* New Haven: Yale UP, 2001.

———. "Technical Communication, Copyright, and the Shrinking Public Domain." *Computers and Composition* 14.3 (1997): 329–42.

Gurak, Laura J., and Ann Hill-Duin. "The Impact of the Internet and Digital Technologies on Teaching and Research in Technical Communication." *Technical Communication Quarterly* 13 (2004): 187–99.

Gurak, Laura J., and Johndan Johnson-Eilola, guest eds. *Computers and Composition* 15.2 (1998).

Harper and Row Publishers, Inc. v. Nation Enterprises, 471 U.S. 539 (1985).

Hawisher, Gail E., and Cynthia L. Selfe. "On Editing and Contributing to a Field: The Everyday Work of Editors." *Pedagogy* 4.1 (2004): 9–26.

Hawke, Constance S. *Computer and Internet Use on Campus: A Legal Guide to Issues of Intellectual Property, Free Speech, and Privacy.* San Francisco: Jossey-Bass, 2000.

hayabusa. "College Republicans from Portland, Oregon, Protest in Support." Web. June 6, 2007. <http://www.youtube.com/watch?v=k-11HM_DZTU>.

Herrington, TyAnna K. *Controlling Voices: Intellectual Property, Humanistic Studies, and the Internet.* Carbondale: Southern Illinois University Press, 2001.

———. *A Legal Primer for Technical Communicators.* New York: Allyn and Bacon/ Longman Publishers, 2003.

———. "Where in the World Is the Global Classroom Project?" *If Classrooms Matter: Progressive Visions of Educational Environments.* Ed. Jeffrey Di Leo and Walter Jacobs. New York: Routledge, 2004. 197–210.

———. "Who Owns My Work? The State of Work-for-Hire for Academics in Technical Communication." *Journal of Business and Technical Communication* 13.2 (1999): 125–53.

———. "Work-for-Hire for Nonacademic Creators." *Journal of Business and Technical Communication* 13.4 (1999): 401–26.

Herrington, TyAnna, and Yuri P. Tretyakov. "The Global Classroom Project: Trouble-Making and Trouble-shooting." In *Online Education: Global Questions, Local Answers.* Ed. Kelli Cargille-Cook and Keith Grant-Davie. Amityville, NY: Baywood Publishers, 2005. 267–83.

Hess, Mickey. Was Foucault a Plagiarist? Hip-hop Sampling and Academic Citation." *Computers and Composition* 23.3 (2006): 280–95.

Hudson, Ashley R. "Can't Get No Satisfaction: The Rise (and Fall?) of Grokster and Peer-to-Peer File Sharing." 59 *Arkansas Law Review* 889 (2007). 889–915.

Hurt, Harry, III. "Oh, to Be 19 and an Entrepreneur" *New York Times*, June 17, 2007.

Hustler Magazine, Inc. v. Falwell. 485 U.S. 46 (1988).

Icarus Project. 1998. Web. 2010. <http://icarus.lcc.gatech.edu/>.

In re Katz. 623 F.2d 122, 126 (2d Cir. 1980).

Jaszi, Peter. "On the Author Effect: Contemporary Copyright and Collective Creativity." *The Construction of Authorship: Textual Appropriation in Law and Literature.* Ed. Martha Woodmansee and Peter Jaszi. Durham, NC: Duke UP, 1994. 29–56.

———. "Toward a Theory of Copyright: The Metamorphoses of 'Authorship.'" 1991 *Duke Law Journal*, 413. 455–502.

Jenkins, Jennifer. "Blackboard Erases Research Presentation with Cease and Desist TRO." Chilling Effects. Sept. 30, 2003. Web. May 24, 2007. <http://www.chillingeffects.org/ weather.cgi?WeatherID=383>.

Johnson v. Schmitz, 119 F. Supp. 2d. 90 (D. Conn. 2000).

Kelly v. Arriba Soft Corporation. 280 F.3d 934 (CA9 2002).

Kessler, Friedrich. "Contracts of Adhesion: Some Thoughts about Freedom of Contract." 43 *Columbia Law Review* 629, 637 (1943).

Keyishian v. Board of Regents. 385 U.S. 589, 603 (1967).

Kienzler, Donna. "Ethics, Critical Thinking, and Professional Communication Pedagogy." *Technical Communication Quarterly* 10.3 (2001): 319–39.

Kinsella, William J. "Rhetoric, Action, and Agency in Institutionalized Science and Technology." *Technical Communication Quarterly* 14.3 (2005): 303–10.

Kugler v. Romain. 58 N.J. 522 (1971).

Lay, Mary M., and William M. Karis. *Collaborative Writing in Industry: Investigations in Theory and Practice*. Amityville, NY: Baywood, 1991.

"LA College Files Defamation Lawsuit against Anonymous Website Contributors." Student Press Law Center. Web. Jan. 13, 2009. <http://www.splc.org/newsflash_archives.asp?id=881&year=2004>.

Laughlin, Gregory Kent. "Who Owns the Copyright to Faculty-Created Web Sites? The Work-for-Hire Doctrine's Applicability to Internet Resources Created for Distance Learning and Traditional Classroom Courses." 41 B. C. L. Rev. 549–84 (May 2000).

Lee, Yong S. *Technology Transfer and Public Policy*. Westport, CT: Quorum Books, 1997.

Liberal Viewer. "Fox News Edits Criticism of McCain Out of *Daily Show* Clip?" Web. Sept. 24, 2009. <http://www.youtube.com/watch?v=ogh6r5ALVMo&feature=fvsr>.

Logie, John. *Peers, Pirates, and Persuasion: Rhetoric in the Peer-to-Peer Debates*. West Lafayette, IN: Parlor P, 2006.

MacMillan, Douglas. Looking over Turnitin's Shoulder. *Business Week Online*. Mar. 13, 2007. Web. June 6, 2007. <http://search.ebscohost.com>.

Malkin, Michelle. "Fair Use Fight: Challenging Universal Music Group." May 9, 2007. Web. May 29, 2007. <http://www.michellemalkin.com/archives/007491.htm>.

Marsh, Bill. "Turnitin.com and the Scriptural Enterprise of Plagiarism Detection." *Computers and Composition* 21.4 (2004): 427–38.

Mattel, Inc. v. MCA Records, Inc. 28 F. Supp. 2d 1120; 1998 U.S. Dist. LEXIS 20943.

McCormick, Brian. "The Times They Are a-Changin': How Current Provisions of the Digital Millennium Copyright Act, Recent Developments in Indirect Copyright Law, and the Growing Popularity of Student Peer-to-Peer File-Sharing Could 'Chill' Academic Freedom and Technological Innovation in Academia." 32 *Journal of College and University Law* 709 (2006). 709–24.

McMillen, John D. "Intellectual Property: Copyright Ownership in Higher Education—University, Faculty, and Student Rights." *College Administration Publications*, 2001. Web. June 6, 2007. <http://search.ebscohost.com>.

McSherry, Corynne. *Who Owns Academic Work? Battling for Control of Intellectual Property*. Boston: Harvard UP, 2003.

Metro-Goldwyn-Mayer Studios, Inc. v. Grokster, Ltd., 380 F.3d 1154 (9th Cir. 2004), vacated 125 S. Ct. 2764 (2005).

Miles, Libby, Jeffrey Galin, Susan Lang, Candace Spigelman, and Michael Moore. "Fair Use Guidelines: Strategies toward Action." *College Composition and Communication* 51.3 (2000): 485–88.

Moneycontrol.com. "Cos Hiring MBA Students to Gain Trade Secrets from Rivals." May 5, 2007. Web. May 24, 2007. <http://www.moneycontrol.com/india/news/business/cos-hiring-mba-students-to-gain-trade-secretsrivals-/279701>.

Muller, Judy. "Plagiarism Goes by a Different Name on the Web." *Nieman Reports* 60.4 (2006): 84–85.

Murray, Charles. "What's Wrong with Vocational School?" *Wall Street Journal*. Web. Aug. 29, 2009. <http://www.opinionjournal.com/extra/?id=110009535>.

Nat'l Med. Care, Inc. v. Espiritu, 284 F. Supp. 2d 424, 434 (S.D.W.Va. 2003).

Nelson, Michael. "The Good, the Bad, and the Phony: Six Famous Historians and Their Critics." *Virginia Quarterly Review* 78.3 (2002): 377–94.

1976 Copyright Act. 17 U.S.C.S. §§ 101–810.

"NYU Student Pulls Website." C-Net News. Apr. 24, 1997. Web. Jan. 13, 2009. <http://news.cnet.com/NYU-student-pulls-Web-site/2100–1023_3–279206.html>.

"Ohio U. Failing Students in RIAA Attack." People to People Net. Web. June 4, 2007. <http://p2pnet.net/story/12340>.

Ornatowski, Cesar M., and Linn K. Bekins. "What's Civic about Technical Communication? Technical Communication and the Rhetoric of 'Community.'" *Technical Communication Quarterly* 13 (2004): 251–69.

Orphan Works Act of 2008. H.R. 5889. Original sponsor: Howard Berman (D-CA 28th). Apr. 24, 2008. 110th Cong., 2d sess. S. 2913. In the House of Representatives, Sept. 27, 2008.

Packard, Ashley. "Copyright or Copy Wrong: An Analysis of University Claims to Faculty Work" 7 *Communication Law & Policy* 275–315 (summer 2002).

Perfect 10 v. Google, 487 F. 3d at 721.

PerSeptive Biosystems, Inc. v. Pharmacia Biotech, Inc., 12 F. Supp. 2d. 69, 71 (D. Mass. 1998).

Pirates of the Caribbean. Disney Film Studios, 2000. Film.

Purdue University. Policy on Intellectual Property. Equities of Participating Parties. XI. 2b. Web. May 25, 2007. <http://www.purdue.edu/policies/pages/teach_res_outreach/b_10.html#inventions>.

Rainey v. Wayne State Univ., 26 F. Supp. 2d 963 (E.D. Mich. 1998).

Reyman, Jessica. "Rethinking Plagiarism for Technical Communication." *Technical Communication* 55.1 (2008): 61–67.

Richardson, Malcolm, and Sarah Ligget. "Power Relations, Technical Writing Theory, and Workplace Writing." *Journal of Business and Technical Communication* 7.1 (1993): 112–37.

Rife, Martine Courant. "The Fair Use Doctrine: History, Application, and Implications for (New Media) Writing Teachers." *Computers and Composition* 24.2 (2007): 154–78.

Rubber-Tip Pencil Co. v. Howard, 87 U.S. (20 Wall.) 498, 507 (1874).

St. Amant, Kirk. "Introduction to the Special Section on Examining International Outsourcing: Perspectives, Practices, and Projections." *IEEE Transactions on Professional Communication* 50 (2007): 81–84.

Samuels, Edward. "The Idea-Expression Dichotomy in Copyright Law." 56 *Tennessee Law Review* 321 (1989).

Samuels, Robert. "The Future Threat to Computers and Composition: Nontenured Instructors, Intellectual Property, and Distance Education." *Computers and Composition* 21.1 (2004): 63–71.

Sandler, Chanani. "Copyright Ownership: A Fundamental of 'Academic Freedom.'" 12 *Albany Legal Journal of Science & Technology* 231–61 (2001).

Sapp, David Alan, and Robbin D. Crabtree. "A Laboratory in Citizenship: Service Learning in the Technical Communication Classroom." *Technical Communication Quarterly* 11 (2002): 411–32.

Savage, Gerald R. "Redefining the Responsibilities of Teachers and the Social Position of the Technical Communicator." *Technical Communication Quarterly* 5 (1996): 309–27.

Selfe, Cynthia L., ed. *Resources in Technical Communication: Outcomes and Approaches*. Amityville, NY: Baywood, 2007.

Selber, Stuart A. *Computers and Technical Communication: Pedagogical and Programmatic Perspectives.* New York: Ablex, 1997.

Seymore, Sean B. "My Patent, Your Patent, Our Patent? Inventorship Disputes within Academic Research Groups." 16 *Albany Law Journal of Science and Technology* 125–67 (2006).

Sharp, Jeff. "Coming Soon to Pay-Per-View: How the Digital Millennium Copyright Act Enables Digital Content Owners to Circumvent Educational Fair Use." 40 *American Business Law Journal* 1 (2002). 2–81.

Slack, Jennifer D., David J. Miller, and Jeffrey Doak. "The Technical Communicator as Author: Meaning, Power, Authority." *Journal of Business and Technical Communication* 7.1 (1993): 12–26.

Slattery, Shaun. "Undistributing Work through Writing: How Technical Writers Manage Text through Complex Information Environments." *Technical Communication Quarterly* 16 (2007): 311–25.

Sonny Bono Copyright Term Extension Act. S 505. Pub. Law 105–298. Oct. 27, 1998.

Sony Corp of America v. Universal City Studios, Inc. 464 U.S. 417 (1984).

Spigelman, Candace. "Gaps and Intersections: Textual Ownership in Theory and Practice." *Across Property Lines: Textual Ownership in Writing Groups.* Carbondale: Southern Illinois UP, 2000.

Stanford University, Stanford Research Administration. Intellectual Property. "Policies." Web. May 25, 2007. <http://www.stanford.edu/dept/DoR/Resources/ip.html#policy>.

Star Wars. 20th Century Fox, 1977–2005. Films.

Stearns, Laurie. "Copy Wrong: Plagiarism, Property, and the Law." 80 *Calif. L. Rev.* 513–53.

TEACH Act. U.S.C. 110(2).

Thralls, Charlotte, and Nancy Roundy Blyler. "The Social Perspective and Pedagogy in Technical Communication." *Technical Communication Quarterly* 2 (1993): 249–69.

Thomas, David A. "How Educators Can More Effectively Understand and Combat the Plagiarism Epidemic." 2004 *Brigham Young University Education and Law Journal* 421. 421–30.

Tillery, Denise. "Power, Language, and Professional Choices: A Hermeneutic Approach to Teaching Technical Communication." *Technical Communication Quarterly* 10 (2001): 97–116.

Time, Inc. v. Bernard Geis Associates. 293. F. Supp. 130 (1968).

Touretzky, D. S. (2000) "Gallery of CSS Descramblers." *Dave Touretzky's Page.* Carnegie Mellon University, School of Computer Science. 2000. Web. May 31, 2007. <http://www.cs.cmu.edu/~dst/DeCSS/Gallery>.

Turnitin. "Turnitin Legal Document." Web. Mar. 12, 2007. <htpp://turnitin.com/static/pdf/us_Legal_Document.pdf>.

Turnitin brochure. Web. June 18, 2007. <http://turnitin.com/static/pdf/Turnitin_brochure.pdf>.

Turnitin.com. Home page. Web. Oct. 21, 2007. <http://www.turnitin.com/static/plagiarism.html>.

Uniform Trade Secrets Act. National Conference of Commissioners on Uniform State Laws. 1985.

University of Minnesota. Intellectual Property. Web. May 25, 2007. <http://www1.umn.edu/regents/policies/academic/IntellectualProperty.html>.

University of Virginia v. VanVoorhies. 342. F.3d 1290 (Fed. Cir. 2003).U.S. Const., art. 1, § 8, cl. 8. Intellectual property provision.

U.S. Copyright Office. Report on Copyright and Digital Distance Education 100 (1999).

Virginia Commonwealth University. Ownership of Intellectual Property. 8. Web. May 25, 2007. <http://www.vcu.edu/provost/univ_policies/intprop.htm>.

West, Joel. "Microsoft to Publishers: We Share the Same Enemy." Web. May 23, 2007. <http://blog.openitstrategies.com/2007/03/microsoft-to-publishers-we-share-same.html>.

Westbrook, Steve, ed. *Composition & Copyright: Perspectives on Teaching, Text-Making, and Fair Use*. Albany: SUNY P, 2009.

Whithaus, Carl, and Joyce Magnotto Neff. "Contact and Interactivity: Social Constructionist Pedagogy in a Video-Based, Management Writing Course." *Technical Communication Quarterly* 15 (2006): 431–56.

Wikipedia. Web. June 11, 2007. <http://en.wikipedia.org/wiki/Wikipedia>.

Williams & Wilkins v. United States. 487. F.2d. 1345 (Ct.Cl. 1973), aff'd per curiam, 420 U.S. 376 (1975).

Index

TyAnna K. Herrington, an associate professor in the School of Literature, Communication, and Culture at the Georgia Institute of Technology, is the author of two books: *Controlling Voices: Intellectual Property, Humanistic Studies, and the Internet* and *A Legal Primer for Technical Communicators*. Herrington, who holds both JD and PhD degrees, was awarded a Fulbright professorship in 1999, which led to her development of the award-winning Global Classroom Project.